The Fairness 'Dilemma' in Sharing the Nile Waters

The Fairness 'Dilemma' in Sharing the Nile Waters

What Lessons from the Grand Ethiopian Renaissance Dam for International Law?

By

Zeray Yihdego

BRILL

LEIDEN | BOSTON

Library of Congress Control Number: 2017940769

Typeface for the Latin, Greek, and Cyrillic scripts: "Brill". See and download: brill.com/brill-typeface.

ISBN 978-90-04-35175-2 (paperback)
ISBN 978-90-04-35176-9 (e-book)

Originally published as Volume 2(2) 2017, in *International Water Law*, DOI 10.1163/23529369-12340006.

This book is printed on acid-free paper and produced in a sustainable manner.

Contents

Acknowledgements

The author is grateful to Abbe Brown, Emily Hirst, Melaku Desta, and the anonymous reviewers for their invaluable comments on earlier versions of the monograph. Thanks are also due to Saloni Sudan for her kind research assistance. Last but not least, I am grateful to my kids, Alexander and Naomi, for giving me love and non-voluntary breaks while working on the monograph.

The monograph builds upon work included in an article published in July 2016: Z. Yihdego, & A. Rieu-Clarke, *An exploration of fairness in international law through the Blue Nile and GERD*, 41 Water International, pp. 528–549 (2016).

The Fairness 'Dilemma' in Sharing the Nile Waters: What Lessons from the Grand Ethiopian Renaissance Dam for International Law?

Zeray Yihdego
School of Law, University of Aberdeen, UK

Abstract

This monograph enquires into the fairness dilemma in connection with the construction of the Grand Ethiopian Renaissance Dam (GERD) in light of relevant colonial-era Nile treaties, post-1990 Nile framework instruments, and international watercourses law. The GERD is now a *fait accompli*, but fairness considerations will continue to be vital issues in its completion, filling, and operation. The monograph argues that the GERD is a symbol of a fair share of the Nile waters by Ethiopia, the realization of which depends on, *inter alia*, an appropriate economic return, benefit sharing and prevention of significant impacts. The monograph also calls for a process to address the issue of unfair agreements, and argues that, although fairness application can be complex, the notions of procedural fairness and distributive justice can be applied to define and delineate the principle with reference to a specific treaty regime.

Keywords

Distributive Justice – GERD – Nile Basin – Procedural Fairness – Watercourses Law

Introduction

Ethiopia's contribution to the Nile waters is attributed to the Sobat (Baro) River, which flows into and contributes almost half of the waters of the White Nile; the Atbara (Tekeze and Angereb) River, which flows into the main stream of the Nile (and contributes 10% of Nile waters); and the Blue Nile, which is the major source of the Nile with about 60% contribution to Nile

 | DOI 10.1163/9789004351769

waters.[1] All these rivers make up more than 86% of Nile waters.[2] The current use of the Nile waters by Ethiopia is negligible; the reasons for such a low use range from a lack of capacity and resources to a bar on the desire to utilize the water resources imposed by a colonial legacy and downstream countries. After a devastating internal civil war lasting three decades until the early 1990s, Ethiopia began to engage in sustainable development efforts, including exploring opportunities to utilize its transboundary rivers for hydro-power generation and other uses.[3] As part of this effort, the Grand Ethiopian Renaissance Dam (GERD), under construction 20 kilometres from the Sudanese border since 2011 on the Blue Nile, was designed to generate 6,000 megawatt (mw) in electricity.[4]

Inside Ethiopia, the GERD is seen as a main driver for prosperity through clean energy generation and as a national symbol. Egypt opposed the project until recently for fear of its impact,[5] but also because of the sentiment attached to the Nile as a historical gift to Egypt.[6] Other Nile riparian countries, including Sudan, now support the construction of the GERD.[7] A western advocacy group, International Rivers Network, opposed the project because of environmental

1 J. V. Sutcliffe & Y. P. Parks, *The Hydrology of the Nile* (Wallingford: IAHS Press, 1999), p. 127, retrieved from http://www.hydrosciences.fr/sierem/produits/biblio/hydrology%20of%20the%20Nile.pdf.

2 Ibid.

3 See, e.g. Ethiopian National Planning Commission, *The Growth and Transformation Plan II* (GTP II), (May 2016), pp. 181–183.

4 See Salini-Impregilo, the GERD contractor's webpage retrieved from http://www.salini-impregilo.com/en/projects/in-progress/dams-hydroelectric-plants-hydraulic-works/grand-ethiopian-renaissance-dam-project.html.

5 Egypt State Information Service, 'Egypt's Perspective towards the Ethiopian Grand Renaissance Dam Project (GERDP),' *allAfrica* (7 December 2015), retrieved from http://allafrica.com/stories/201512072751.html.

6 Constitution of the Arab Republic of Egypt, 18 January 2014, retrieved from http://www.sis.gov.eg/Newvr/Dustor-en001.pdf. Article 44 reads:

The State shall protect the River Nile, preserve Egypt's historical rights thereto, rationalize and maximize its use, and refrain from wasting or polluting its water. The State shall also protect groundwater; adopt necessary means for ensuring water security; and support scientific research in that regard.

Every citizen is guaranteed the right to enjoy the River Nile. It is prohibited to trespass the riverbank reserve or harm the riverine environment. The State shall guarantee eliminating any trespass against the River Nile as regulated by Law.

7 S. Salman, 'The Ethiopian Renaissance Dam: Opportunities & Challenges,' *Sudanow Magazine* (20 September 2013), retrieved from http://sudanow.info.sd/the-ethiopian-renaissance-dam-opportunities-challenges/.

concerns,[8] while others from Africa and elsewhere consider it as 'a symbol of Regional Integration'[9] and 'an opportunity for collaboration and shared benefits in the Eastern Nile Basin.'[10]

The dam has been a source of tension between Egypt and Ethiopia[11] up until Egyptian President Al-Sisi came to power in June 2014. Subsequently, a series of painstaking negotiations among the three countries culminated in the adoption of the 'Declaration of Principles between The Arab Republic of Egypt, the Federal Democratic Republic of Ethiopia and the Republic of the Sudan on the Grand Ethiopian Renaissance Dam Project' ('DoPs') in March 2015.[12]

The path to concluding the DoPs was hindered by perceived legal claims and counterclaims as well as differences over facts. Despite fundamental disagreements between Egypt and Ethiopia, a series of talks were held among the parties which led to the establishment of the International Panel of Experts (IPoE) in May 2012, at the initiation of Ethiopia, to study the effects of the dam on Egypt and Sudan and to build confidence among the parties. The IPoE, constituted of two experts each from Egypt, Sudan and Ethiopia and a further four international experts, published its final report on 31 May 2013. The report is not publicly available in full, and, at the time, was interpreted by Egypt as a 'confirmation' of its concerns that the GERD will 'significantly harm' its interests.[13] Ethiopia strongly felt it was 'vindicated' by the report as the Panel ruled out

---

8 *The Grand Ethiopian Renaissance Dam Fact Sheet*, International Rivers Network, retrieved from http://www.internationalrivers.org/resources/the-grand-ethiopian-renaissance-dam-fact-sheet-8213.

9 *The Grand Ethiopian Renaissance Dam—A Symbol of Regional Integration*, Ventures Africa (4 March 2014), retrieved from http://www.ventures-africa.com/archives/40137.

10 See MIT Abdul Latif Jameel World Water and Food Security Lab, *The Grand Ethiopian Renaissance Dam: An Opportunity for Collaboration and Shared Benefits in the Eastern Nile Basin*, (2014), retrieved from http://jwafs.mit.edu/sites/default/files/documents/GERD_2014_Full_Report.pdf [MIT Report].

11 M. B. Kelley & R. Johnson, 'STRATFOR: Egypt is Prepared to Bomb All of Ethiopia''s Nile Dams,' *Business Insider* (13 October 2012), retrieved from http://www.businessinsider.com/hacked-stratfor-emails-egypt-could-take-military-action-to-protect-its-stake-in-the-nile-2012-10#ixzz3afm498Zg.

12 Agreement on Declaration of Principles between the Arab Republic of Egypt, the Federal Democratic Republic of Ethiopia and the Republic of the Sudan on the Grand Ethiopian Renaissance Dam Project (GERDP), 23 March 2015 [DoPs], retrieved from http://hornaffairs.com/en/2015/03/25/egypt-ethiopia-sudan-agreement-on-declaration-of-principles-full-text/

13 Egypt State Information Service, supra 'note 5, p. 2.

the possibility of significant harm, and instead emphasized the shared benefits and increased water flow from the GERD.[14]

The aftermath of the DoPs is largely dominated by a spirit of cooperation and mutual trust among Ethiopia, Sudan and Egypt. Although the DoPs is founded on modern legal principles of international watercourses law, old legal arguments are neither expressly denounced nor recognized in the Declaration. The DoPs was followed by the signing of the Khartoum minutes[15] in December 2015 in which the parties reiterated their continued commitment to the DoPs, and also agreed to hire two French consultancy firms, BRLi Group and Artelia, to help them understand the downstream impacts of the GERD.[16] This led to the signing of a contract between the three countries and the two firms in September 2016 to conduct studies on 'Water Resources/Hydropower System Simulation Model and Transboundary Environmental and Socio-economic Impact Assessment'[17] of the GERD. The precise scope, nature and purpose of the studies are not publicly known; the firms' work is to be finalized within 11 months from the end of 2016,[18] which may well be after the two GERD turbines begin generating electric power[19] and the major structures of the dam are complete and ready for dam reservoir filling.[20] However, these studies, in particular the hydropower system simulation model, may be of vital use and help 'in the negotiations on the period of filling the GERD reservoir'[21] if the parties use of them as a positive resource of cooperation rather than contention.

---

14 D. Berhane, "Ethiopia' Dismisses International Rivers as Egypt's Proxy,' *Horn Affairs English* (11 April 2014), retrieved from http://hornaffairs.com/en/2014/04/11/ethiopia-dismisses-international-rivers-as-egypts-proxy-full-text-included/

15 S. Salman, 'The Grand Ethiopian Renaissance Dam: The Road to the Declaration of Principles and the Khartoum Document,' *Water International* Vol. 41(4) (2016), pp. 512–527, p. 512.

16 Ibid., p. 523.

17 S. Goshu, 'BRLi, Artelia Get Clearance to Conduct GERD Impact Studies,' *Ethiopian Reporter* (24 September 2016).

18 See, 'Egypt, Ethiopia, Sudan Sign Final Contracts on Nile Dam Studies,' *Ahramonline* (20 September 2016), retrieved from http://english.ahram.org.eg/News/244290.aspx.

19 'GERD to Start Generate 750 MW Soon,' *EBC* (15 October 2015), retrieved from http://www.ebc.et/web/ennews/-/gerd-to-start-generate-750-mw-soon.

20 Y. Zhang, S. Erkyihum & P. Block, 'Filling the GERD: Evaluating Hydroclimatic Variability and Impoundment Strategies for Blue Nile Riparian Countries,' *Water International* Vol. 41(4) (2016), pp. 593–610, p. 594. These hydrologists predict that filling of the GERD 'is likely to begin as early as 2018.

21 Salman, supra note 15, p. 524.

While the tripartite meetings on the GERD have been on-going in a positive spirit of promoting mutual interest of the three countries, the late 2016 civil unrest in Ethiopia led the latter to accuse Egypt, or some Egyptian institutions, of backing the violent protests in Ethiopia. Ethiopian President Mulatu Teshome in his address to Parliament on 10 October 2016 asserted that 'groups and individuals which our country describe as terrorists like the Oromo Liberation Front and the Ginbot 7, work hand in hand with Egyptian institutions and are responsible for the recent destruction in our country.'[22] Egyptian President Al-Sisi swiftly denied the Ethiopian allegation saying, 'Egypt does not conspire against anyone.'[23] He went on 'to assure our brothers in Ethiopia that Egypt has never ever offered any support to the opposition and will not carry out any conspiratorial action against Ethiopia.'[24] While this makes the Ethio-Egyptian relations politically fluid,[25] 'the three countries have officially agreed to continue negotiations on the GERD'; the Ethio-Sudanese relationship in particular is thriving as Sudan plans 'to build a 3,000 megawatt power transmission line from the GERD' to its cities.[26]These topical but complex developments, coupled with the controversies surrounding old and post-1990 Nile 'commitments', make the GERD a unique example of the fairness dilemma in scholarly enquiry.

In light of these developments in the Nile Basin, this monograph examines three legal questions relating to the principle of fairness. The first concerns whether the GERD's (un)fairness can be judged on the basis of relevant colonial-era treaties, the 1902 (Anglo-Ethiopian) and the 1959 Nile treaties in particular.[27] The second concerns whether the 1993 Framework Agreement

---

22 E. Boh, 'Ethiopia Accuses Egypt of "'Fueling'" Violence,' *Africanews* (10 October 2016), retrieved from http://www.africanews.com/2016/10/10/ethiopia-accuses-egypt-of-fueling-violence/.

23 A. Abdelatti, 'Egypt's Sisi Denies Supporting Opposition in Ethiopia,' *Reuters* (13 October 2016), retrieved from http://uk.reuters.com/article/uk-ethiopia-unrest-egypt-idUKKCN12D2L5.

24 Ibid.

25 A. Zaher, 'Egypt-Ethiopia Tension Set to Rise,' *The Arab Weekly*, Issue 78 (23 October 2016), p. 9.

26 See 'Sudan to Build Power Transmission Line from Ethiopia's GERD: Minister,' *Sudan Tribune* (28 October 2016), retrieved from http://www.sudantribune.com/spip.php?article60680.

27 As discussed below (*infra* 'Colonial-era Treaties and the Fairness of the GERD'), the 1902 Nile Treaty is referred to as a colonial-era treaty since Britain, one of the parties to the treaty, was in control of both Sudan and Egypt. Moreover, although the 1959 Nile Waters Agreement was concluded by the two independent states of Egypt and the Sudan, it is referred to as a colonial-era treaty in this monograph because most of the other Nile

between Egypt and Ethiopia and the 2015 DoPs provide a fair justification for the construction and operation of the GERD. The final question is whether the GERD in general, and the DoPs in particular, will have legal implications for basin-level cooperation under or outside the Nile Basin Cooperative Framework Agreement (CFA) and international watercourses law more generally. Put differently, are there lessons to be learnt from the case study for international law more generally? These and related questions cannot be tackled without explaining the nature of the principle of fairness.

The Principle of Fairness

Features and Challenges

Thomas Franck's pioneering work on fairness,[28] though not the first to introduce the subject,[29] argued in favour of an emerging legal principle of fairness in international law. Furthermore, he argued, this principle could be applied to the allocation of resources, and might cover both procedural elements and distributive justice. The procedural aspect of fairness, as a legal concept, deals with participation and the involvement of concerned parties in the formulation and development of legal rules which legitimize both law-making and implementation processes.[30] Conversely, distributive justice, as a moral notion, deals with the essence, content and impact of laws on people, communities and states.[31] This is to be determined in light of history and societal context, and is subject to the 'moderate scarcity' of resources, 'community' and 'reciprocity.'[32] Due to these characteristics two principal caveats were proposed to the fairness discourse. Firstly, absolute or non-negotiable claims over contentious rights and duties must be rejected, and secondly, inequality can be tolerated or recognized as a matter of fact so long as such an inequality

---

riparians were still under colonial domination. African states were by and large under colonial rule at the time, and the decolonization process only began in the 1960s. See, e.g., Declaration on the Granting of Independence to Colonial Countries and Peoples, 14 December 1960, Resolution 1514 (XV), United Nations General Assembly.

28 T. Franck, *Fairness in International Law and Institutions* (Oxford: Clarendon Press, 1995).

29 J. A. Rawls, 'Justice as Fairness,' *The Philosophical Review*, Vol. 67(2) (1958), pp. 164–194.

30 Franck, supra note 28, pp. 7–8 and 25.

31 Ibid., pp. 8–9.

32 Ibid., pp. 8–15. Franck underlined the need for an agreement on 'a core of reciprocally applicable rules' (p. 12). 'Moderate scarcity' refers to 'a finite, non-renewable,' particularly something in 'short global supply' (p. 9). 'Community' is 'a social system of continuing interaction and transaction. It is only in a community that the bedrock of shared values and developed principles necessary to any assessment of fairness is found.' (pp. 9–10).

ultimately serves fairness and thus aims to narrow an existing gap between the beneficiary and the deprived.[33] When applying the fairness discourse to international law, the proposition rightly assumes the existence of international law as a mature legal system that is subject to continuous negotiations, compromises and reasoning to achieve a 'perceived fairness' by concerned parties on a specific subject matter, such as resource allocation.[34] This notion of fairness is seen by some as utopian,[35] but by others as a justified and necessary principle in the international community.[36] The latter position seems to be the dominant view, as will be shown below in relation to international watercourses law.

There is, however, no definition or description of what the principle is precisely in the fairness discourse. Judge Owada,[37] in his separate position in the *Wall Advisory Opinion*, submitted that

> [c]onsideration of fairness in the administration of justice requires equitable treatment of the positions of both sides involved in the subject-matter in terms of the assessment both of facts and of law involved.[38]

This is in line with the common perception that fairness is synonymous with equity and justice[39] and thus shares their definition. In Roman (domestic) law, justice is seen as "the set and constant purpose which gives to every man his due.'[40] This appears to focus on substance rather than process or procedure. In contrast, for John Rawls, justice is 'the first virtue of social institutions, as truth is of systems of thought.... [L]aws and institutions no matter how efficient

33 Ibid., pp. 16–18.

34 Ibid., p. 14.

35 J. Tasioulas, 'International Law and the Limits of Fairness,' *European Journal of International Law*, Vol. 13(4) (2002), pp. 993–1023; I. Scobbie, 'Tom Franck's Fairness,' *European Journal of International Law*, Vol. 13(4) (2002), pp. 909–925.

36 D. Kritsiotis, 'Imagining the International Community,' *European Journal of International Law*, Vol. 13(4) (2002), pp. 961–992, p. 968; D. Shelton, 'Equity',' *in*, D. Bodansky, J. Brunnée & E. Hey (eds.), *The Oxford Handbook of International Environmental Law*, pp. 640–661 (Oxford: Oxford University Press, 2007), pp. 645–649.

37 *Legal Consequences of the Construction of a Wall in the Occupied Palestinian Territory*, Advisory Opinion of 9 July 2004, Separate Opinion of Judge Owada, [2004] ICJ Reports, pp. 260–271.

38 Ibid., p. 260.

39 Shelton, supra note 36, p. 640.

40 J. B. Moyle, *The Institutes of Justinian, 5th ed.* (Oxford: Clarendon Press, 1913), bk I, title 1, retrieved from http://droitromain.upmf-grenoble.fr/Anglica/just1_Moyle.htm.

and well-arranged must be reformed or abolished if they are unjust.'[41] Evidently, from this definition, justice does not appear to have any meaning without fairness (and equity) and vice versa. The emphasis placed on 'institutions' and effectiveness in defining fairness and justice raises the question whether the two concepts have been perceived restrictively to procedural and institutional questions. In contrast, Grotius diligently clarifies that justice is presumed to be denied only when it is delayed but also where a 'judgement has been rendered in a way manifestly contrary to law.'[42] Hence, according to Grotius, deviating from or complying with laws, amongst other things, constitutes the idea of (in) justice. Again, it is not clear whether his reference to the law is meant to embrace both procedure and substance.

Steven Ratner's definition, which goes beyond national law, describes

> global justice *as process or outcome that assigns rights and duties to global actors so that it is clear what each such actor is entitled or required to do or have*. Norms of international law are just if they assign those rights and duties in a way that meets a substantive standard of justice.[43]

This definition of justice clearly captures both procedure and the content of laws.

Equity, in contrast to justice, implies a general principle of law, filling gaps in the law, not applying unjust laws, and adaptable interpretation and application of laws to particular cases.[44] Indeed, this approach to equity appears to be broader in scope, comprising both processes and substantive matters, and possibly, going beyond the law in applying ethical and moral imperatives. For this reason, the nature of equity has been more controversial. One view broadly sees equity as 'subjective appreciation' of facts and laws in dealing with legal claims and counterclaims,[45] while another view, which resembles Grotius' view on justice, considers equity as 'an expression of an objective

---

41 J. A. Rawls, *Theory of Justice*, rev. ed. (Cambridge, MA: Harvard University Press, 1999), p. 3.

42 H. Grotius, *The Law of War and Peace, Book III, Chapter 2, Vol. 1* (1625). Retrieved from http://lonang.com/library/reference/grotius-law-war-and-peace/gro-302/

43 R. S. Ratner, *The Thin Justice of International Law: A Moral Reckoning of the Law of Nations* (Oxford: Oxford University Press, 2015), p. 44. Italics in the original.

44 M. Akehurst, 'Equity and General Principles of Law,' *International and Comparative Law Quarterly*, Vol. 25(4) (1976), pp. 801–825, pp. 801–802; O. McIntyre, 'Utilization of Shared International Freshwater Resources: The Meaning and Role of "Equity" in International Water Law,' *Water International*, Vol. 38(2) (2013), pp. 112–129, pp. 114–117.

45 R. Jennings, 'Equity and Equidistance Principles,' *Annuaire Suisse de Droit International*, Vol. 27 (1986), pp. 31–35, pp. 27 & 31.

idea of justice.'[46] From this one may deduce that justice and equity are either different sides of the same coin or that equity is a tool that can, or ought to, be used to articulate justice, with justice being the ultimate objective of applying laws.

Despite the broader nature of equity and its close relationship, to say the least, with justice,[47] the International Court of Justice (ICJ) detached it from the notion of 'distributive justice'[48] without clear explanation. In contrast, Steven Ratner, building on Herbert Hart's conception of justice, writes 'in thinking about justice as relational [between different claimants' of rights/duties], it seems like we cannot escape the idea of distributions, or more precisely of allocations....'[49]

Misleadingly, the debate over distributive justice is often framed in international law in the context of the North-South divide and the question of a legal or moral duty to the share resources between developed and developing members of the international community.[50] While there is a merit in this debate, it is not within the scope of this monograph. Further, it seems to overlook distributive justice's wider appeal beyond such a divide, for example, in relation to resource sharing among members of the same category (developed or developing countries), a historical or current specific injustice by a member of one category against a member of the other category, and special legal regimes such as international watercourses law. With this in mind, this monograph aims to probe the justifiability of the outright rejection or support for distributive justice as a legal concept.

Given that the concepts of justice, equity and fairness are inherently interweaven with each other, this monograph explores their nature by applying John Rawls'[51] thesis that 'the fundamental idea in the concept of justice is fairness,'[52] in all its aspects and caveats, including distributive justice, as

---

46 *Case Concerning Pulp Mills on the River Uruguay (Argentina v Uruguay)*, Judgment of 20 April 2010, Separate Opinion of Judge Trindade, [2010] ICJ Reports, paras. 10 & 11 [*Pulp Mills*].

47 V. Lowe, 'The Role of Equity in International Law,' *Australian Yearbook of International Law*, Vol. 12 (1988–89), pp. 54–81, p. 54; Akehurst, supra note 44.

48 *Case Concerning the Continental Shelf (Tunisia/Libyan Arab Jamahiriya)*, Vol. 1, Judgment of 24 February 1982, [1985] ICJ Reports 13, para. 71.

49 Ratner, *supra* note 43.

50 M. Prost& A. T. Camprudi, 'Against Fairness? International Environmental Law, Disciplinary Bias and Pareto Justice,' *Leiden Journal of International Law*, Vol. 25(2) (2012), pp. 379–396, p. 379.

51 Rawls, supra note 29.

52 Ibid., p. 164.

meticulously articulated in Franck's[53] fairness discourse. Franck has not defined the principle of fairness, and it must be recognized that the application of fairness, justice and equity may well vary from one field to another depending on relevant laws and the objectives therein. The principle of fairness, for the purpose of this monograph, will imply a system of 'fair dealing' or 'fair play'[54] in relations among sovereign states, which includes transboundary resource sharing, with the aim of attaining legally acceptable, proportionate and just, as opposed to arbitrary and unequal, processes and results.[55] This general description of fairness only serves as a starting point in the application of the concept to specific cases and problems.

Before applying the principle to international watercourses law, however, a few points merit consideration here. The characterization of distributive justice by Franck as a moral or ethical, rather than legal, concept is troubling. Of course, laws and regulations are informed by (im)moral underpinnings; further, substantive matters in fields ranging from international trade and economic law and the law of the sea, to that of armed conflict and human rights are not matters of abstract ethical standards. However, the fairness discourse has not denied the embodiment of substantive rules of equity as fairness onto treaties and conventional arrangements, as this monograph will illustrate.

Similarly, while socio-economic or other forms of inequality (or inequity) are a fact, be it in the relations between individuals or states, their open endorsement in international law, conceptually or normatively, defeats the core values and foundations of international law, including the principles of sovereign equality and permanent sovereignty over natural resources.[56] It may well be that the fairness discourse takes into account existing situations, including

---

53 Franck, supra note 28.

54 M. Maiese, 'Principles of Justice and Fairness,' *in*, G. Burgess & H. Burgess (eds.), *Beyond Intractability* (Boulder: Conflict Information Consortium, University of Colorado, 2003), retrieved from http://www.beyondintractability.org/print/2373.

55 R. Wolfrum, 'Commentary on Purposes and Principles (Art 1),' *in*, B. Simma et al., *The Charter of the United Nations: A Commentary, 3rd ed., Volume 1,* pp. 113–114 (Oxford: Oxford University Press, 2012), pp. 113–114; *Tunisia/Libyan Arab Jamahiriya Case*, supra note 49, para. 71; *Case Concerning the Gabčikovo-Nagymaros Project (Hungary v Slovakia)*, Judgement of 25 September 1997, [1997] ICJ Reports 7, para. 147; Z. Yihdego & A. Rieu-Clarke, 'An Exploration of Fairness in International Law Through the Blue Nile and GERD,' *Water International*, Vol. 41(4) (2016), pp. 528–549.

56 Charter of Economic Rights and Duties of States, 12 December 1974, Resolution 3281 (XXIX), United Nations General Assembly, Arts. 2, 8 & 10.

inequality, as one factor for determining or promoting distributive justice,[57] which is not the same as recognizing such disparity as a matter of principle. The elements of 'community' of states and resource 'scarcity,' as part of the principle at issue, are persuasive and imperative; the addition of 'reciprocity' as a condition to the fairness discourse can, however, be supported or challenged; some cases and claims associated with transboundary resources can be of an *erga omnes* and not of a reciprocal character.[58] Yet reciprocity remains crucial in inter-state relations, including in the governance of transboundary resources for the purposes of promoting equity and mutual interest among countries.[59]

There is hardly a uniform definition or a universally shared perception of the principle of fairness, however it is named, and, as a result, scholars question its existence as a legal concept in international law.[60] While sharing and acknowledging these qualms, the fairness discourse argues that there is an emerging recognition of equity as fairness in international case law and treaty law.[61] At the very least, it is argued, fairness constitutes a general principle of law as recognized in Article 38(1)(c) of the ICJ Statute.[62] The following section applies the principle of fairness to international watercourses law through the well-developed concept of equity.

---

57 Ibid., Art. 25; see also The Marrakesh Agreement Establishing the World Trade Organization, 1994, 1869 *UNTS* 299. The first preambular paragraph of the Agreement promotes, *inter alia*, 'optimal use of the world's resources ... in a manner consistent with their [States] respective needs and concerns at different levels of economic development.' This appears to acknowledge and accept the economic and development levels of WTO member States. The second preambular paragraph, however, emphasizes the 'need for positive efforts designed to ensure that developing countries, and especially the least developed among them, secure a share in the growth in international trade commensurate with the needs of their economic development.'

58 *Case Concerning the Barcelona Traction, Light and Power Company, Limited (Belgium v Spain)*, Second Phase Judgment of 5 February 1970, [1970] ICJ Reports 3. See also Ratner, supra note 43, pp. 59–62.

59 *The Diversion of Water from Meuse (Netherlands v Belgium)*, PCIJ Series A/B No 70 (28 June 1937) [*Diversion of Water*].

60 P. Malanczuk, *Akehurst's Modern Introduction to International Law, 7th ed.* (Cheltenham: Routledge, 1997), pp. 54–55; I. Brownlie, *Legal Status of Natural Resources in International Law (Some Aspects) (Volume 162)* (Leiden: Brill Nijhoff, 1979), p. 288.

61 Franck, supra note 28, pp. 79–80.

62 Ibid., pp. 47–79.

Relevance to Watercourses Law in General

Equity as fairness comes with different categories including 'corrective equity' and 'broadly conceived equity.'[63] The latter is a rule-based equity established by a specific treaty or policy regime.[64] Franck used the draft of the Convention on the Law of the Non-Navigational Uses of International Watercourses 1997 (UNWC)[65] as one example of applying fairness. He argued that the 'distributive justice' can be attained by considering relevant factors including socio-economic situations in riparian states for the purposes of determining an 'equitable apportionment of river water' on a case-by-case basis.[66] Nearly 20 years later from when the fairness discourse sparked a serious debate among scholars, the UNWC entered into force in August 2014; the basic rights and duties enshrined in the Convention also reflect customary international law.[67] In this sense, Franck's contribution to the fairness debate in international law more generally, appears to have borne fruit, although this process has not without challenges.

The fact that the distinction between procedural and substantive law is not always a clear-cut case may offer a challenge or an opportunity for fairness. The UNWC reflects both the opportunities and challenges of the fairness discourse, consisting of detailed and complex substantive and procedural rules on the sharing and protection of transboundary water resources. The principle of equitable and reasonable utilization,[68] which tends to be a favourite of upstream

63 Ibid., pp. 56–75; Lowe, *I* note 48, pp. 54–58; O. McIntyre, *Environmental Protection of International Watercourses under International Law* (Aldershot: Ashgate, 2007), p. 120.

64 Franck, supra note 28, pp. 65–66.

65 Convention on the Law of the Non-navigational Uses of International Watercourses, 21 May 1997, entered into force 17 August 2014, United Nations General Assembly, Resolution 51/229 (8 July 1997), 36 *ILM* 700 (1997) [UNWC]. For some background on the Convention see, 'The International Law Commission Draft Articles on the Law of the Non-navigational Uses of International Watercourses 1994,' International Legal Commission, retrieved from http://legal.un.org/ilc/texts/instruments/english/commentaries/8_3_1994.pdf.

66 Franck, supra note 28, pp. 74–75.

67 *Case Relating to the Territorial Jurisdiction of International Commission of the River Oder (United Kingdom v Poland)*, PCIJ Series A No 23, Annex 3 (Order made on 20 August 1929), p. 27; *Hungary v Slovakia*, supra note 55, para. 85; McIntyre, supra note 63, p. 112; B.-O. Magsig, *International Water Law and the Quest for Common Security* (Cheltenham: Routledge, 2015), p. 49.

68 UNWC, supra note 65, Arts. 5 & 6.

countries,[69] and the duty not to inflict significant harm[70] as a subordinate to the equitable principle, which is generally favoured by downstream countries,[71] constitute the core elements of distributive justice. However, international watercourses law is not merely about sharing and utilizing water resources. The protection and preservation of watercourses and their natural environment[72] as a legal principle constitutes part of distributive justice.[73] The scope of this substantive duty under the UNWC has been articulated by Salman as follows:

> The Convention establishes a number of obligations on the watercourse states, including protection and preservation of ecosystems; prevention, reduction and control of pollution; introduction of alien or new species; and protection and preservation of the marine environment. A Statement of Understanding issued by the [UN General Assembly Sixth Committee] Working Group clarified that these provisions impose a due diligence standard on watercourse states.[74]

The UNWC reconciles the principle of environmental protection with the principle of equitable utilization on two grounds. First, as enshrined under Article 5, the equitable principle obliges watercourse states to take 'into account the interests of the watercourse States concerned, consistent with adequate protection of the watercourse.' Second, as enshrined in Article 6(1) of the Convention, equitable utilization must take into account factors such as socio-economic needs, impacts of water use, current and potential use, and

69 S. Salman, 'Entry into Force of the UN Watercourses Convention: Why Should it Matter?,' *International Journal of Water Resources Development*, Vol. 31(1) (2015), pp. 4–16, p. 9. DOI: 10.1080/07900627.2014.952072.

70 UNWC, *supra* note 65, Art. 7. It has been clarified, however, that downstream countries can also harm upstream countries. See, e.g., S. Salman, 'Downstream Riparians Can Also Harm Upstream Riparians: The Concept of Foreclosure of Future Uses,' *Water International*, Vol. 35(4) (2010), pp. 350–364.

71 Salman, *supra* note 69.

72 UNWC, *supra* note 65, Arts. 20–26; P. Birnie, A. Boyle & C. Redgwell, *International Law and the Environment, 3rd ed.* (Cambridge: Cambridge University Press, 2009), pp. 535–582.

73 S. McCaffrey, *The Law of International Watercourses, 2nd ed.* (Oxford: Oxford University Press, 1997), pp. 387–463; Magsig, *supra* note 67.

74 Salman, *supra* note 69, p. 10.

'conservation, protection, development and economy of use of the water resources of the watercourse and the costs of measures taken to that effect.'[75]

However, the factors set out in Article 6 might be criticized for lacking empirical guidance and arguably for not being objectively determinable. As Professor Dellapenna reflects upon, however,

> Non-lawyers, particularly engineers and hydrologists, sometimes see in these catalogues of factors a poorly stated equation. By this view, if one simply fills in numerical values for each factor, one could somehow calculate each watercourse state's share of the water without reference to political or other non-quantitative variables. They simply ignore that the UN Convention … and the Helsinki Rules [on the Uses of the Waters of International Rivers] are legal documents that ultimately are addressed to judges. Judges make judgements, and in the English language, at least, the word judgement carries a strong connotation that the result is not dictated in any immediate sense by the factual and other inputs that the judge relies upon in exercising judgement. Any attempt to treat the list of relevant factors as an algorithm simply misses the point entirely.[76]

---

75 UNWC, *supra* note 65, Art. 6(1)(f); the full list of factors is:
(a) Geographic, hydrographic, hydrological, climatic, ecological and other factors of a natural character;
(b) The social and economic needs of the watercourse States concerned;
(c) The population dependent on the watercourse in each watercourse State;
(d) The effects of the use or uses of the watercourses in one watercourse State on other watercourse States;
(e) Existing and potential uses of the watercourse;
(f) Conservation, protection, development and economy of use of the water resources of the watercourse and the costs of measures taken to that effect;
(g) The availability of alternatives, of comparable value, to a particular planned or existing use.

76 J. W. Dellapenna, 'The Customary International Law of Transboundary Fresh Waters,' *International Journal of Global Environmental Issues*, Vol. 1 (3–4) (2001), pp. 264–305, p. 287.

Article 6 of the UNWC further reinforces this by clarifying that

> [t]he weight to be given to each factor is to be determined by its importance in comparison with that of other relevant factors. In determining what is a reasonable and equitable use, all relevant factors are to be considered together and a conclusion reached on the basis of the whole.[77]

Hence, the principle of equitable utilization serves as an umbrella and primary principle in applying distributive justice, and embraces the environmental protection and no significant harm principles.[78] Furthermore, the umbrella principle of international watercourses law and the factors necessary to determine equity are subject 'to consultations in a spirit of cooperation,'[79] which suggests that they can only be applied on a case-by-case basis depending on natural, man-made and other features of a watercourse. It follows from this that the equitable utilization primary principle along with its subordinate norms and factors, as enshrined in the UNWC, truly aligns to the notion of distributive justice for two simple reasons: (i) it deals with the content and essence of the law the application of which impacts states, communities and individuals; and (ii) the factors listed to determine the equitable principle further reinforce Franck's proposition that distributive justice should be determined by the relevant history and social context. Furthermore, the caveats and conditions to distributive justice fit into international watercourses law in that water resources are scarce, and competition over them has become fierce; there is no place for absolute or non-negotiable claims in the UNWC as required in the fairness discourse. However, one cannot say with certainty that inequality is tolerated in international watercourses law. The UNWC refers to 'existing and potential use' as one factor for determining equitable use, but the Convention neither endorses nor rejects existing inequality of use among riparian states. Another notable difference is that while the international watercourses law principles and factors are legally endorsed standards, the fairness discourse sees distributive justice as a moral notion. Such moral standards can, however, be integrated into legal instruments, as Franck himself acknowledges by referring to the terms of the (draft) UNWC.

---

77 UNWC, supra note 65, Art. 6(3). This needs to be read in conjunction with Article 10, which suggests that no use has an inherent priority.

78 Salman, supra note 70, p. 354.

79 UNWC, supra note 65, Art. 6(2).

In contrast to distributive justice, the duty, *inter alia*, to cooperate,[80] notify and consult,[81] exchange data and information,[82] and dispute settlement provisions of the UNWC[83] are procedural in character.[84] The duty 'to enter into consultations' has been extended to managing 'an international watercourse, which may include the establishment of a joint management mechanism'[85] and 'planning the sustainable development of an international watercourse and providing for the implementation of any plans adopted.'[86] Most importantly, the legal entitlement to participate in law making of watercourse states has been duly recognized under Article 4(1) of the UNWC:

> Every watercourse State is entitled to participate in the negotiation of and to become a party to any watercourse agreement that applies to the entire international watercourse, as well as to participate in any relevant consultations.

This is extended to any agreement which 'applies only to a part of the watercourse or to a particular project' if the implementation of such an agreement may significantly affect a watercourse state's legal interests.[87] Worthy of note is that Article 5 is also about equitable participation.

These and other procedural aspects of the UNWC cover activities ranging from participation in law making to participation in institutional and formal processes and mechanism through which agreed legal standards are realized. This is very much in line with the procedural fairness concept of Franck. Unlike distributive justice, international watercourses law and Franck's procedural fairness concept concern legal (rather than moral) arrangements. However, such categorization can be misleading as some of the principles, such as the equitable utilization and participation, and the duty to take all appropriate measures to prevent significant harm, are both substantive and procedural in

80 UNWC, supra note 65, Art. 8. Article 25(1) of the Convention provides: 'Watercourse States shall cooperate, where appropriate, to respond to needs or opportunities for regulation of the flow of the waters of an international watercourse.'

81 Ibid., Arts. 12–18 & 24.

82 Ibid., Arts. 9 & 11–19.

83 Ibid.

84 McCaffrey, supra note 73, pp. 464–481.

85 UNWC, supra note 65, Art. 24(1).

86 Ibid., Art. 24(2)(a).

87 Ibid., Art. 4(2). See also Article 25(2) which provides: 'Unless otherwise agreed, watercourse States shall participate on an equitable basis in the construction and maintenance or defrayal of the costs of such regulation works as they may have agreed to undertake.'

nature.[88] Furthermore, as briefly mentioned above, the application of the factors set out in Article 6(1) of the UNWC to determine equitable use require consultation and cooperation among concerned states as per the second paragraph of the same Article. Similarly, the legal commitment on the management of watercourses has not only dealt with procedural matters but also with 'promoting the rational and optimal utilization, protection and control of the watercourse,'[89] which are elements of the equitable utilization and participation principle. This needs to be read with caution as the overlaps between distributive justice and procedural fairness do not fundamentally eliminate the natural boundary between the content and procedure of law.

Undoubtedly, customary international law governing shared watercourses, as represented by the UNWC,[90] provides the right platform to exhibit both the merits and challenges of the fairness discourse. Despite the strong suggestion that some of the core rules of watercourses law constitute customary international law, and thus bind all states in respect of all international watercourses, the Convention has only been ratified by 36 states and applies to those who subscribe to it as far as *treaty* rights and duties are concerned. This adds to the complexity of applying the principles to all watercourses cases, in particular the procedural provisions that are key for a fair deal in using and protecting shared watercourses. Regardless, international watercourses law demonstrates that the notion of distributive justice can be found in special legal regimes of international law, which appears to challenge its unexplained rejection, including by the ICJ, as shown above.

The UNWC is a general instrument, and states parties to the Convention are thus allowed (and may also be encouraged) under Article 3(3) to enter into 'watercourse agreements' that 'apply and adjust the provision of the present Convention to the characteristics and uses of a particular international watercourse or part thereof.' The implementation and elaboration of the rules and principles enshrined in the UNWC on a case-by-case basis would appear to be more appropriate, if not absolutely required and, in this Article's case, at

88 McCaffrey, supra note 73, p. 401; A. Rieu-Clarke & G. Pegram, 'Impacts on the International Architecture for Transboundary Waters,' *in*, F. R. Loures & A. Rieu-Clarke, *The UN Watercourses Convention in Force: Strengthening International Law for Transboundary Water Management*, pp. 67–76 (Abingdon: Routledge, 2103).

89 UNWC, supra note 65 above, Art. 24 (2) (b).

90 S. Salman, 'The Helsinki Rules, the UN Watercourses Convention and the Berlin Rules: Perspectives on International Water Law,' *International Journal of Water Resources Development*, Vol. 23(4) (2007), pp. 625–640, pp. 625–640; *Hungary v Slovakia*, supra note 55, para. 85.

sub-basin level. However, it is appropriate to first consider basin-wide endeavours in implementing these rules.

Relevance to an Emerging Nile Basin Legal Framework

At present, none of Nile Basin countries are parties to the UNWC, which makes the search for (un)fairness in Nile water sharing difficult, if not impossible. This is because the Convention is not applicable to them without their consent. Countries of the Basin do however rely on established principles of the law including the ones recognized in and promoted by the UNWC, as discussed below, albeit selectively, to substantiate their claims and counterclaims.[91]

More broadly, Nile Basin-level initiatives have endorsed the aforementioned principles of international watercourses law. Negotiated within the Nile Basin Initiative (NBI)[92] framework, which is a transitional arrangement,[93] the Cooperative Framework Agreement (CFA)[94] aims to promote cooperation, equality, optimal and sustainable use of Nile waters, and sustainable development.[95] Articles 8, 10 and 12 of the CFA deal with the principles of information exchange on planned measures, data and information exchange, and peaceful settlement of disputes respectively, which can be considered as dominantly procedural commitments. The CFA also aims to establish a Nile River Basin Commission comprising heads of state and government, a Council of Ministers, a Technical Advisory Committee, a Sectoral Advisory Committee and the Secretariat to manage and administer effective cooperation among Basin states, including the sharing of information on planned measures.[96]

The substantive duties of the CFA are similar, if not identical, to those of the UNWC and include the principles of equitable use,[97] preventing significant

91 See 'Colonial-era Treaties and the Fairness of GERD' and 'Post-1990 Nile Instruments: A Way Out of the Fairness Dilemna?' in this monograph.

92 S. Salman, 'The Nile Basin Cooperative Framework Agreement: A Peacefully Unfolding African Spring?,' *Water International*, Vol. 38(1) (2013), pp. 17–29, pp. 19–20.

93 Ibid.

94 Agreement on the Nile River Basin Cooperative Framework, May 2010, retrieved from http://www.nilebasin.org/images/docs/CFA%20-%20English%20%20FrenchVersion.pdf [CFA]. Seven countries agreed for the text to be opened for signature; six countries, namely Ethiopia, Kenya, Uganda, Burundi, Rwanda and Tanzania have signed the Agreement; Ethiopia, Tanzania and Rwanda have ratified it. The CFA requires six ratifications for its entry into force, at which time it will replace the NBI. Retrieved from http://www.nilebasin.org/index.php/spotlight/99-cfa-overview.

95 Ibid., Art. 1.

96 Ibid., Arts. 8 & 15–17.

97 Ibid., Art. 4.

harm[98] and protecting and conserving water resources.[99] Interestingly, however, unlike the UNWC, the CFA refers to the principles of 'subsidiarity'[100] and 'community of interest'[101] of Nile Basin states; these are meant to promote an equitable share and sustainable use of water resources but also create a sense of community in the sharing of the benefits and responsibilities relating to Nile waters and its ecosystem. Worthy of particular mention is the duty of Basin states deduced from the principle of subsidiarity to 'allow all those within a State who will or may be affected by the project in that State to participate in an appropriate way in the planning and implementation process.'[102] Similar to the law in other river basins such as the Lake Victoria Basin,[103] the Danube,[104] and the European Union[105] in general, this approach recognizes the participation (or/and the right to information) of non-state actors in the use and protection of river basin waters.

It can be argued that, although it does not explicitly deal with non-state actors' participation, the UNWC contains similar principles to that of the CFA, as shown in Articles 5, 6 and 7 as considered above; yet elements such as water contribution to a river basin as a factor to determine reasonable use[106] appears to be, justifiably[107] or unjustifiably,[108] not explicitly included in the UNWC. Furthermore, 'the extent and proportion of the drainage area in the

---

98 Ibid., Art. 5.

99 Ibid., Art. 7.

100 Ibid., Art. 3.

101 Ibid., Art. 9.

102 Ibid., Art 10(a). This follows from the main principle and commitment enshrined under Article 3(3) that 'development and protection of the Nile River Basin water resources is planned and implemented at the lowest appropriate level.'

103 Protocol for Sustainable Development of Lake Victoria Basin, 29 November 2003, Art. 3(i) retrieved from http://faolex.fao.org/docs/pdf/mul41042.pdf.

104 Convention on the Cooperation for the Protection and Sustainable Use of the Danube River, 29 June 1994, entered into force 22 October 1998, OJ L342 (12 December 1997), Art. 14, retrieved from https://www.icpdr.org/main/icpdr/danube-river-protection-convention.

105 EU Water Framework Directive, 2000/60/EC, 23 October 2000. Paragraph 46 states that '[t]o ensure the participation of the general public including users of water in the establishment and updating of river basin management plans, it is necessary to provide proper information of planned measures and to report on progress with their implementation with a view to the involvement of the general public before final decisions on the necessary measures are adopted.'

106 CFA, supra note 94, Art. 4.

107 McIntrye, supra note 63, pp. 182–183.

108 The Helsinki Rules on the Uses of the Waters of International Rivers, August 1966, International Law Association, Art. V(b).

territory of each Basin State[109] has been listed as one of the criterion for equitable sharing of water resources of a basin under the CFA, but not in the UNWC. According to this parameter, those states that have a larger drainage area within a river basin, which may not necessarily imply making more or less water contribution to a river basin, have an advantage over those who have smaller basin drainage areas, although as enshrined in CFA Article 4(4) 'the weight to be given to each factor is to be determined by its importance in comparison with that of other relevant factors'. The CFA does not claim to be exhaustive[110] with its list of factors, which is broadly, but not identically, the case with the UNWC.[111] Notably, the GERD's DoPs boldly endorsed water contribution and the size or proportion of drainage area as factors to be taken into account in applying the principle of equitable use of Nile waters.[112]

As part of the water security concept the CFA introduced 'the right of all Nile Basin States to reliable access to, and use of, the Nile River system for health, agriculture, livelihoods, production and the environment';[113] this concept is not explicitly mentioned in the UNWC. The concept of water security was intended to bridge the differences between downstream and upstream countries[114] and thus provide a symbol of fairness and equality. However, it has been criticized for trying to introduce a non-legal concept[115] to a legal instrument dealing with a complex issue. Water security appears to be derived from the concept of 'human security,' which is by and large seen as a policy concept rather than a legal one.[116]

---

109 CFA, *supra* note 94, Art 4(i).

110 Ibid., Article 4(2) begins with 'including but not limited to the following,' before listing the factors to be used for applying the equitable principle of water utilization.

111 UNWC, supra note 65, Article 6, in comparison to the CFA, begins with 'including' in listing the factors of the equitable principle.

112 DoPs, supra note 12.

113 CFA, supra note 94, Arts. 2(f) & 14.

114 Salman, supra note 92, p. 21.

115 D. Z. Mekonnen, 'The Nile Basin Cooperative Framework Agreement Negotiations and the Adoption of a "Water Security" Paradigm: Flight into Obscurity or a Logical Cul-de-sac?,' *European Journal of International Law*, Vol. 21(2) (2010), pp. 421–440. DOI: 10.1093/ejil/chq027.

116 Z. Yihdego, 'Arms Control and Human Security: What Role for NSAs?,' *in*, C. Ryngaert & M. Noortmann, *Human Security and International Law: The Challenge of Non-State Actors*, pp. 135–174 (Cambridge: Intersentia, 2014).

Arguably, the CFA is 'a peacefully unfolding African spring'[117] for the following reasons. First, the Agreement, which comprises procedural and substantive principles that are basically similar, but not identical, to the UNWC, is an emerging legal regime. Secondly, most Nile Basin states subscribe to it and thus it represent the hopes and fears of a majority of concerned parties. Finally, the CFA can be seen as declaratory of existing legal principles and rules in the field. However, Egypt and Sudan are not signatories for fear that their historic water rights will be affected and that the majority of participants will dominate decisions on projects.[118] This is a bar to the emergence of Basin-level effective cooperation.[119] It is also detrimental to riparian states on matters of information exchange of planned measures via the Nile Basin Commission, although this does not equate to the duty of prior notification as enshrined in Articles 12–18 of the UNWC.[120] This has led some to consider the CFA as untenable and for calls to negotiate a new legal regime for the Nile.[121] The main barriers for progress appear to be lack of political will, an inability to compromise and low levels of mutual trust which may, or may not, be resolved through the CFA or a newly agreed legal framework.

The CFA, either as an emerging treaty regime or a declaration of existing legal principles in international watercourses law, will be vital to addressing questions of fairness with respect to Nile water sharing. However, the unwillingness of Egypt and Sudan to endorse the Framework renders the initiative less relevant to the fairness discourse. This is not because of the unfairness of the terms of the CFA, but the fact that an agreement is a cardinal prerequisite of a fair system. Consideration of other relevant instruments, including Nile colonial-era treaties, thus, becomes imperative in the search for the fairness of the GERD.

117 Salman, supra note 92, pp. 17–29.

118 Centre of Judicial Studies and Research of the State Council, 'Final Recommendations of the Conference on Nile Basin Agreements in Light of the Provisions of the International Law,' *African Perspectives*, Vol. 11(39) (2013), pp. 68–70.

119 S. O. McKenzie, 'Egypt's Choice: From the Nile Basin Treaty to the Cooperative Framework Agreement, an International Legal Analysis,' *Transnational Law & Contemporary Problems*, Vol. 21 (2012), pp. 571–599, p. 571ff, retrieved from http://papers.ssrn.com/sol3/papers.cfm?abstract_id=2445962.

120 Salman, supra note 92, p. 21.

121 M. Kimenyi & J. Mbaku, *Governing the Nile River Basin: The Search for a New Legal Regime* (Arlington: Brookings Institution Press, 2015), pp. 83–89.

Colonial-era Treaties and the Fairness of the GERD

The Anglo-Ethiopian Treaty 1902 and the GERD

The 1902 Nile Treaty is amongst the key colonial treaties which were, and still are, invoked by Egypt[122] to oppose the construction of any project on major Nile tributaries stemming from Ethiopia. This agreement, signed by Ethiopia with colonial Britain (on behalf of Sudan), stipulated that Ethiopia must 'not construct or allow to be constructed any work across the Blue Nile, Lake Tana, or the Sobat, which would arrest the flow of their waters'[123] without consent from Britain and Sudan.

With respect to the GERD, Shetewy[124] understands the 1902 Treaty as 'Ethiopia's commitment to preserve Egypt's historical rights.'[125] It is not clear why the Treaty is opposable to Ethiopia by Egypt as the latter was not a party to it, although it should be read in conjunction with other treaties that were meant to protect Egyptian (and to some degree Sudan's) 'historic rights.' The 1929 Nile Treaty, which was concluded between colonial Britain (on behalf of Sudan) and Egypt, not only allocated 48 and 4 billion cubic metres (BCM) of Nile waters per annum for Egypt and Sudan respectively, but also went on to impose Basin-wide duties, as enshrined in paragraph 4(b) of the Treaty:

> Except with the prior consent of the Egyptian Government, no irrigation works shall be undertaken nor electric generators installed along the Nile and its branches nor on the lakes from which they flow if these lakes are situated in Sudan or in countries under British administration which could jeopardize the interests of Egypt either by reducing the quantity of water flowing into Egypt or appreciably changing the date of its flow or causing its level to drop.

---

122 See, e.g., Egyptian Perspectives, supra note 6, p. 4. The 2014 document asserts that 'the conduct of the Ethiopian government is inconsistent with its obligations according to the 1902' Nile treaty.

123 Treaties between the United Kingdom and Ethiopia, and between the United Kingdom, Italy, and Ethiopia, relative to the frontiers between the Soudan, , Ethiopia and Eritrea, Addis Ababa, 15 May 1902, Art. III retrieved from http://treaties.fco.gov.uk/docs/pdf/1902/TS0016.pdf [1902 Nile Treaty].

124 M. A. Shetewy, 'Legal Commitments Regulating the Establishment of Water Projects on International Rivers Application Study over the Nile Basin,' *African Perspectives*, Vol. 11(39) (2013), pp. 29–35.

125 Ibid., pp. 34–35.

Similarly, the bilateral Nile Treaty signed between Egypt and Sudan in 1959 divided the entire Nile water flow at 55.5 and 18.5 BCM per year respectively, excluding evaporation at the Aswan High Dam reservoir. The 1959 and the 1929 Nile Treaties raise several questions, including their fairness to the parties themselves. More specifically, while assessing the question of their fairness to Sudan (or Egypt) is not within the realm of this monograph, their impact on perceived duties (and rights) of upstream countries, including on Ethiopia, is certainly relevant here.

McCaffrey,[126] citing Lauterpacht as an authority, sees the 1929 and 1959 Treaties as legal engagements that are designed to share Nile waters that reach Sudan and Egypt. He further submits that these two treaties were meant neither to create obligations upon upstream countries nor to endorse Egyptian 'prior apportionment.' However, according to Shaw, colonial boundaries are not subject to alteration (also known as *uti possidetis juris*), irrespective of 'their arbitrary and alien character.'[127] Article iii of the 1902 Treaty was part of a boundary treaty. If one looks into the history of the provision, however, it is clear that it was separately negotiated for about three years to protect British Nile interests prior to its insertion into the 1902 Treaty at the last minute.[128] More importantly, as the article concerns restricting work on a transboundary river rather than including a piece of land, lake or territorial waters to a state's sovereign territory, it is doubtful that the subject of Article iii belongs to boundary delimitation.[129] There is no evidence that African states meant to include colonial laws and policies with respect to transboundary resources within the concept of 'respect of borders existing on achievement of independence.'[130]

Although *uti possidetis* was widely endorsed by tribunals as a means of avoiding territorial disputes in Africa and elsewhere,[131] its scope and nature

126 McCaffrey, supra note 73, p. 266.

127 M. Shaw, 'The Heritage of States: The Principle of uti possidetis juris Today,' *British Yearbook of International Law*, Vol. 67(1) (1996), pp. 75–154, pp. 97 & 104.

128 T. W. Woldetsadik, *International Watercourses Law in the Nile River Basin: Three States at a Crossroads* (Abingdon: Routledge, 2013), p. 100; A. H. Garretson, 'The Nile Basin,' *in*, A. H. Garretson, R. D. Hayton & C. J. Olmstead (eds.), *The Law of International Drainage Basins*, pp. 256–297 (New York: Oceana, 1967), p. 277.

129 Shaw, *supra* note 127, p. 77.

130 Constitutive Act of the African Union, 11 July 2000, Art. 4(b), retrieved from https://au.int/web/sites/default/files/pages/32020-file-constitutiveact_en.pdf. See also Cairo Declaration on Border Disputes among African States Legitimising National Borders Inherited from Colonial Times, Organization for African Unity, 1964, paras. 1 & 2.

131 *Case Concerning the Frontier Dispute* (*Burkina Faso/Republic of Mali*), Judgment of 22 December 1986, [1986] ICJ Reports 554, para. 20.

was associated with the 'issue of acquisition of title to territory' and *terra nullius* (i.e. nobody's land) territories.[132] Judge Yusuf argues strongly that 'none of the official documents of the OAU [Organisation of African Unity] or of its successor organization, the AU [the African Union], relating to African conflicts, territorial or boundary disputes, refers to or mentions in any manner the principle of *uti possidetis juris*'[133] and it is therefore a legally different concept from what Article 4 of the AU constitutive act prescribes. Whatever the legal position of *uti possidetis* in Africa and elsewhere, its invocation with respect to shared watercourses' use, outside the context of boundary lines that are needed to limit 'territorial jurisdiction of states,'[134] is a misreading of the principle at best, or an attempt to evade state sovereignty, which embraces authority over their resources, at worst.

Yet maintaining the Nile *status quo* is imperative to the peace and stability of the region—changing the current use of Nile waters without consent of all concerned is therefore not only illegitimate but destabilizing.[135] Even when one endorses keeping the *status quo* argument, the question remains whether such a justification should be followed at the expense of the basic rights of others on a shared watercourse.[136]

Further, Article iii of the 1902 Nile Treaty is seen as an invalid and the Treaty has not been ratified by Ethiopia,[137] but is binding and applicable for Egypt.[138] Arguably, the latter's position may be challenged or supported based upon the notion of fundamental change of circumstances (also known as *rebus sic stantibus*) as a ground to terminate or withdraw from a treaty obligation, as expressly recognized under Article 62 of the Vienna Convention on the Law

---

132 *Frontier Dispute* (*Burkina Faso/Niger*), Judgement of 16 April 2013, Separate Opinion of Judge Yusuf, [2013] ICJ Reports, p. 137, para. 11, retrieved from http://www.icj-cij.org/docket/files/149/17312.pdf.

133 Ibid., p. 136, para. 10.

134 S. Ratner, 'Drawing a Better Line: UTI Possidetis and the Borders of New States,' *American Journal of International Law*, Vol. 90(4) (1996), pp. 590–624, p. 602.

135 P. L. O. Lumumba, 'The Interpretation of the 1929 Treaty and its Legal Relevance and Implications for the Stability of the Region,' *African Sociological Review*, 11(1) (2007), pp. 10–24, pp. 7–18.

136 Permanent Sovereignty Over Natural Resources, 14 December 1962, Resolution 1803 (XVII), United Nations General Assembly.

137 J. H. S. Lie, *Supporting the Nile Basin Initiative: A Political Analysis 'Beyond the River'*, Norwegian Institute of International Affairs (2010), p. 7, revived from: http://www.academia.edu/2243972/Supporting_the_Nile_Basin_Initiative_A_Political_Analysis_Beyond_the_River.

138 Egyptian Perspective, *supra* note 5.

of Treaties 1969 (CVLT).[139] This article sets out stringent requirements such as a change of radical nature and the non-application of *rebus sic stantibus* to boundary treaties, which might support the argument that Ethiopia is not entitled to terminate or withdraw from Article iii obligations of the 1902 Treaty.[140]

Decolonisation in Africa and elsewhere, and the political and territorial changes in the Sudan[141] and Ethiopia, may challenge the non-application of *rebus sic stantibus* as a ground to invalidate Article iii of the 1902 Treaty. Developments in the law including the CFA regime,[142] the non-objection by Egypt and Sudan to the Tekezé Dam[143] that was completed in 2009 on a Nile tributary to supply electricity to both Ethiopia and Sudan, and now the acceptance of the GERD by Sudan and Egypt mean that the current situation is fundamentally different[144] from that of 1902. Alternatively, Egypt and Sudan has wilfully withdrawn, by implication or otherwise, their claims,[145]as the aforementioned developments suggest. For these reasons therefore Article iii of the

139 Vienna Convention on the Law of Treaties, 23 May 1969, 1155 *UNTS* 331 [VCLT]. Article 62 reads:

1. A fundamental change of circumstances which has occurred with regard to those existing at the time of the conclusion of a treaty, and which was not foreseen by the parties, may not be invoked as a ground for terminating or withdrawing from the treaty unless:
   a. The existence of those circumstances constituted an essential basis of the con sent of the parties to be bound by the treaty; and.
   b. The effect of the change is radically to transform the extent of obligations still to be performed under the treaty.
2. A fundamental change of circumstances may not be invoked as a ground for terminating or withdrawing from a treaty:
   a. If the treaty establishes a boundary; or.
   b. If the fundamental change is the result of a breach by the party invoking it either of an obligation under the treaty or of any other international obligation owed to any other party to the treaty.
3. If, under the foregoing paragraphs, a party may invoke a fundamental change of circumstances as a ground for terminating or withdrawing from a treaty it may also invoke the change as a ground for suspending the operation of the treaty.

140 A. Salama, 'The Principle of Fundamental Change in Circumstances and its Impact on the Nile Basin Agreements,' *African Perspectives*, Vol. 11(39) (2013), pp. 36–40.

141 Woldetsadik, supra note 128, p. 116.

142 T. Tvedt, *The River Nile in the Post-colonial Age: Conflict and Cooperation in the Nile Basin Countries* (London: I. B. Tauris & Co, 2009), p. 10; McCaffrey, supra note 74, pp. 271–271.

143 'Ethiopia Inaugurates Africa's First Ever Biggest Power Dam,' *Sudan Tribune* (14 November 2009).

144 VCLT, *supra* note 139, Art. 62(1)(a)–(b).

145 Tvedt, supra note 142, pp. 10–11.

1902 Nile Treaty has been terminated,[146] if not *void ab initio*. This is a particularly powerful argument as Sudan, on whose behalf Article iii was agreed, is now a strong backer of the GERD and other Ethiopian dams.[147] For the reasons discussed above, the argument that Article iii forms a boundary treaty in the context of Article 62 of the VCLT is without legal validity and might amount to an abuse of *rebus sic stantibus*.[148] This is evident from the drafting history of Article 62 with reference to boundary treaties:

> The 1963 Drafting Committee proposed the formula: "a treaty establishing a territorial settlement", a phrase which like Waldock's [ILC Special Rapporteur on the VCLT] draft was intended to cover not only a transfer of territory itself but also ancillary rights arising from the transfer. This proved not to be acceptable to the majority which wished to avoid any reference to the grant of territorial rights and to limit the exception to treaties which either established a territorial boundary or actually transferred territory.[149]

This perhaps provides a relatively clear indication of the limited scope of 'boundary treaties' in the context of the exclusion of their application to the *rebus sic stantibus*-based invocation of terminating a treaty obligation.

Even so, and as outlined above, dozens of Nile colonial-era treaties, including the 1959 Nile Treaty concluded between Egypt and Sudan, unambiguously aimed at the 'full utilization of the Nile waters'[150] by both Egypt and Sudan.

---

146 VCLT, supra note 139, Art. 59(1).

147 A. Eleiba, 'Sudanese President Backs Ethiopian Dam Ahead of Nile Talks,' *Ahramonline* (5 December 2013), retrieved from http://english.ahram.org.eg/News/88321.aspx.

148 When Article 62 of the VCLT was debated at the United Nations in 1968, Libya, amongst non-western European countries, warned that the vague notion of fundamental change of circumstances could be abused by states. The United States, amongst others, was very critical of the concept. See E. Schwelb, 'Fundamental Change of Circumstances,' *in*, *Comments on the 1968 Draft Convention on the Law of Treaties*, pp. 39–70 (Heidelberg: Max-Planck-Institut für ausländisches öffentliches Recht und Völkerrecht, 1999), p. 47, retrieved from http://www.zaoerv.de/29_1969/29_1969_1_c_39_70.pdf.

149 Ibid., p. 55 (footnotes omitted). The ILC did also clarify that '[b]y excepting treaties establishing a boundary from its [Article 62] scope the present article would not exclude the operation of the principle of self-determination in any case where the conditions for its legitimate operation existed' (ibid, p. 58).

150 United Arab Republic and Sudan Agreement (with Annexes) for the Full Utilization of the Nile Waters, 8 November 1959.

This treaty was concluded despite the fact that Ethiopia served notice in 1957 that it would pursue unilateral development of the Nile water resources within its territory.[151] By the same token, the 1929 Nile Treaty, which was committed to by Great Britain on behalf of its east African colonies, was rejected not only by Ethiopia but also by Sudan, Tanzania, Burundi and Kenya.[152] Some states gave a grace period of two years from independence to negotiate on the fate of Nile and other colonial treaties entered into on their behalf; it was declared that after the lapse of such a period the treaties were presumed to be terminated. This is often referred to as the Nyerere Doctrine.[153].

To recap, the 1902 Nile Treaty coupled with the 1929 and 1959 colonial-era treaties have been used by both downstream and upstream countries to defend their existing monopoly and demands for a fair share of the Nile waters.[154] However, the validity and current application of these treaties has been seriously challenged. The 1959 Nile Treaty is unique in that it is not a colonial treaty *per se*, although as it was founded on the purpose and object of its predecessor, and a number Nile Basin countries were still colonized when it was concluded. It could be said that it is closer to Nile colonial treaties than contemporary international watercourses law. Even if these treaties are said to still be applicable, the question of their fairness remains. The following section analyses the fairness of these treaties and their implications for the GERD in the light of what has been considered so far and other issues of treaty law such as the law of succession.

151 McCaffrey, supra note 73, p. 269; G. T. Degefu, *The Nile: Historical, Legal and Developmental Perspectives* (New York: Trafford Publishing, 2003), p. 99.

152 R. K. Paisley & T. W. Henshaw, 'Transboundary Governance of the Nile River Basin: Past, Present and Future,' *Environmental Development*, Vol. 7 (July 2013), pp. 59–71, pp. 59 & 63.

153 A. Okoth-Owiro, 'State Succession and International Treaty Commitments: A Case Study of the Nile Water Treaties,' Occasional Paper, East Africa # 9, Konrad Adenauer Stiftung and Law & Policy Foundation (2004), pp. 13–21, retrieved from http://www.kas.de/wf/doc/kas_6306-544-1-30.pdf. As discussed below, the Nyerere Doctrine was named after the position taken by the first prime minister of independent Tanganyika (later Tanzania), Julius Nyerere, on the Nile issue. He did not believe that Tanganyika is not bound by Nile colonial treaties unless the obligations form part of customary international law. E. B. Kasimbazi, 'The Impact of Colonial Agreements on the Regulation of the Waters of the River Nile,' *Water International*, Vol. 35(6) (2010), pp. 718–732. DOI:10.1080/02508060.2010.533642; Salman, *supra* note 92, p. 18.

154 McCaffrey, supra note 73, p. 270.

The GERD*'s Fairness in the Eyes of Colonial Treaties*

As Franck diligently put it:

> Achieving a shared perception of fairness is much harder than thinking up a formula, but no formula can legitimate a mandatory regime of allocation which is not perceived as fair by those whose conduct it is meant to regulate. In this lies the existential opportunity, the pragmatic imperative. Fairness is the only basis for allocation on which 'everyone' is likely to agree.[155]

The implications of colonial treaties for the fairness debate and dilemma are analysed with this powerful quote in mind. Procedurally, Ethiopia is arguably bound by the 1902 Nile Treaty. Ethiopia was an independent sovereign state who 'agreed' not to 'arrest' Nile waters or construct any projects on the tributaries of the river and thus is bound by the Treaty.[156] However, the circumstances of concluding that treaty, including its ambiguity and the subsequent rejection and non-ratification by Ethiopia, rendered it void from the outset.[157] Most importantly, the British Empire, as a party to the Treaty, ceased to exist decades ago. Thus invoking it today against the GERD is procedurally flawed.

Egypt and Sudan might argue that they are justified in invoking the 1902 Treaty to oppose the GERD as successors of colonial Britain,[158] which is supported by the 'continuity' doctrine of legal commitments.[159] The law of treaty succession[160] appears to be clear that all (bilateral) treaties, especially those which lack universal appeal, are not assumed to be succeeded by independent or newly created states, a position supported by the 'clean state' or 'non-devolution' doctrine.[161] Most, if not all, Nile Basin countries, as former colonies

155 Franck, supra note 28, p. 13.

156 M. S. Aal, 'Equitable and Reasonable Utilization of International Rivers in the UN Convention with a Particular Reference to the River Nile,' *African Perspectives*, Vol. 11(39) (2013), pp. 22–28, p. 27.

157 See 'The Anglo-Ethiopian Treaty 1902 and the GERD' in this mongraph.

158 A. Abulwafa, 'Commitment of International Conventions on the River Nile,' *African Perspectives*, Vol. 11(39) (2013), pp. 7–13.

159 M. C. R. Craven, 'The Problem of State Succession and the Identity of States under International Law,' *European Journal of International Law*, Vol. 9 (1998), pp. 142–162, p. 147.

160 VCLT, supra note 139, Art. 16.

161 T. Maluwa, *International Law in Post-Colonial Africa* (Leiden: Martinus Nijhoff, 1999), p. 69; C. Leb & M. Tignino, 'State Succession to Water Treaties: Uncertainties and Extremes,' *in*, L. B. Boisson de Chazournes, C. Leb & M. Tignino (eds.), *International Law*

of Britain, rejected Nile colonial-era treaties, which comprise the Sudan.[162] In particular, the 1961 Declaration of Tanganyika on succession of the 1929 Treaty articulates both the rejection of that treaty and the need for starting a fresh process based upon negotiation, reciprocity and equity. The Declaration reads as follows:

> The Government of Tanganyika has come to the conclusion that the provisions of the 1929 Agreement purporting to apply to the countries 'under British Administration' are not binding on Tanganyika. At the same time, however, and recognizing the importance of the waters of the Nile that have their source in Lake Victoria to the Government and peoples of all the riparian states, the Government of Tanganyika is willing to enter into discussions with other interested Governments at the appropriate time, with a view to formulating and agreeing on measures for the regulation and division of the waters in a manner that is just and equitable to all riparian states and of the greatest benefits to all their peoples.[163]

This position, which is elaborated on in procedural and time period terms, as discussed above, was followed by other countries that were former colonies, and is strong evidence of the 'clean state' doctrine of state succession. This doctrine may not apply, however, to (independent) Ethiopia regarding the 1902 Nile Treaty because it was not colonized like the others. Yet the unevenness of the deal between a mighty colonial power and a country under exigent threat from different colonial powers makes such an argument untenable.[164] Conversely, Sudan, on whose behalf the 1902 Treaty was concluded, was a colony of Britain, and thus a beneficiary of the clean state doctrine, an entitlement which was exercised by Sudan against the 1929 Nile Treaty.[165] Whether Sudan will formally and expressly abandon colonial treaties as a legal basis for its Nile water entitlement remains to be seen.[166] If Sudan expressly or impliedly renounces the application of the 1902 Nile Treaty, however, it will be apparent that Egypt will not have legitimate ground to rely on that treaty for the purpose of objecting to current or future projects upstream, including the

and Freshwater: The Multiple Challenges, pp. 421–444 (Cheltenham: Edward Elgar, 2013), p. 425.

162 McCaffrey, supra note 73, p. 270.

163 As quoted in Mekonnen, supra note 115, p. 434.

164 Degefu, supra note 151, p. 99.

165 McCaffrey, supra note 73, p. 269.

166 Salman, *supra* note 92.

GERD. It may be said that Egypt (and Sudan) have impliedly renounced the 1902 Nile Treaty by officially endorsing the GERD; however, this contradiction will remain unless the 1902 Treaty is expressly denounced by Egypt as a legal ground to question projects upstream. It is unlikely that the 1959 Nile Treaty is relevant to the law of state succession involving other Nile riparians, arguably excepting South Sudan. It is of note that the law of treaty succession was not meant to retain earlier illegal treaties.[167]

In summary, these are largely procedural questions ranging from rules of treaty making to that of state succession (and *uti possidetis*), the primary legal basis of which has been the 1902 Nile Treaty. However, this 104 years old treaty was not procedurally fair, like other Nile colonial treaties, and therefore does not provide a sound legal basis on which to reject the GERD as procedurally unfair. This does not inevitably render Article iii of the Treaty substantively unfair and the GERD fair.

Substantively, some authors aiming to protect the historic use 'rights' of Egypt, to which the Nile is seen as lifeblood,[168] maintain that the 1902 and the 1929 and 1959 Nile Treaties are fair. The desert state's population relies on this river for drinking, fishing, agriculture, hydropower and tourism. However, it is also fair to say that Nile colonial-era treaties, including the 1902 Treaty, like other colonial treaties, were instigated by the self-interest of colonial powers rather than the shared interest of the community of Nile riparian states. For this reason, and despite the claim of pursuing 'a civilising mission,' such colonial treaties have been 'discontinued in international law' as substantively flawed and discriminatory treaties.[169] Importantly, the treaties at issue here conflict with the right to self-determination of peoples in upstream countries and their entitlement to fair use and utilization of the river's resources, while their tributaries contribute every drop of Nile waters, and thus defeat the notion of distributive justice.[170]

It appears that the British Empire recognized such injustice as early as the 1950s, and began to question the absolute ownership of the Nile by downstream countries, particularly by Egypt. The 1959 UK declaration on Nile waters submits that

---

167 Ratner, supra note 134, p. 600; *Hungary v Slovakia*, supra note 55.

168 E.g., Aal, supra note 156, p. 27.

169 A. Boyle & C. Chinkin, *The Making of International Law* (Oxford: Oxford University Press, 2009), pp. 28–29.

170 Z. Yihdego, *The Blue Nile Dam Controversy in the Eyes of International Law*, Global Water Forum, retrieved from http://www.globalwaterforum.org/2013/06/18/the-blue-nile-dam-controversy-in-the-eyes-of-international-law/.

> the territories of British East Africa will need for their development more water than they at present use and will wish their claims for more water to be recognised by other states concerned. Moreover, they will find it difficult to press ahead with their own development until they know what new works downstream States will require on the headwaters within British East African Territory. For this reason, the United Kingdom Government would welcome an early settlement of the whole Nile waters question.[171]

This declaration only concerns Uganda, Kenya and Tanganyika, all former colonies of the British Empire, but Ethiopia, as a legitimate stakeholder in matters of Nile waters, was also publicly referred to by British authorities as early as 1956. For example, MP James Johnson (of Rugby) stressed in parliamentary debate on 18 May 1956

> the enormous significance the future establishment of a Nile Valley Authority could have for people, black and white alike, in *Ethiopia*, Uganda, Tanganyika and Kenya. It is a bold and imaginative project. The conservation of the waters of the Nile opens up an exciting future for the people of those parts.[172]

Although there is no evidence of any official policy to address the interests of Ethiopia with respect to Nile waters, this quote shows that there was some discussion about, and recognition of, Ethiopia's interests in British establishments.

Both the downstream and upstream countries believe, or claimed to have believed, in fair use of Nile waters. Their views on the fairness of relevant colonial treaties reflect this—the treaties considered above are claimed to be fair in protecting historic and prior water use of downstream countries, but unfair from upstream countries' perspective. This is evidence of the fairness dilemma in sharing and protecting Nile water resources as the very same treaties are often relied upon to make a fair use argument and to protect existing use of Nile waters. Hence, the treaties at issue are not that helpful to judge the (un) fairness of the GERD as fairness is about agreeing on fundamental principles that duly take into account the legal rights and interests of all parties. The two

---

171 A. H. Garretson, 'The Nile River System,' *Proceedings of the American Society of International Law*, Vol. 54 (1960), pp. 136–163, p. 143.

172 552 Parl. Deb., H.C. (5th ser.) (18 May 1956) cc2375–412 (Nile Waters), sec 2395, italics added. Retrieved from http://hansard.millbanksystems.com/commons/1956/may/18/nile-waters#column_2395.

post-1990 Nile framework instruments provide better insights into the fairness of the GERD, and therefore are considered next.

Post-1990 Nile Instruments: A Way Out from the Fairness Dilemma?

The 1993 Framework Instrument

The Framework for General Co-operation between the Arab Republic of Egypt and Ethiopia[173] (Framework Instrument) was signed by presidents Hosni Mubarak of Egypt and Meles Zenawi of Ethiopia in July 1993 in Cairo. Ethiopia was led by a Transitional Government established under the *Transitional Period Charter of Ethiopia* 1991.[174] In contrast, although with its own serious internal challenges, including Islamic extremism, repression and an economic crisis, Egypt was under the leadership of a long-serving president and (relatively) strong, *inter alia*, in its diplomatic, institutional and human capacity,[175] which are crucial to promoting a state's legal and political interests. As the discussion below will reveal, it is not clear whether the Framework Instrument was signed in good faith (also known as *bona fides*) by the parties to it as required by international (watercourses) law.[176] Moreover, it is not clear whether it was a hastily or a well-thought-out negotiated political/legal undertaking.

The Framework Instrument duly signed by the two heads of state recognized the need for realizing 'their full economic and resource potential' and underlined that both states have a 'mutual interest' in the Nile Basin.[177] The principles of 'good neighbourliness,' 'peaceful settlement of disputes,' 'non-interference' in their internal affairs,' 'mutual trust and understanding,' and 'promoting economic and political interests,' including regional stability, are laid out in the Instrument.[178] These founding principles were followed by

173 Framework for General Co-operation between the Arab Republic of Egypt and Ethiopia, 1 July 1993, UNTS, Vol. 2693, No. 47816, retrieved from http://gis.nacse.org/tfdd/tfdddocs/521ENG.pdf [1993 Framework Instrument].

174 *Negarit Gazeta*, 1991–07–22, Vol. 50, No. 1 [Ethiopia], pp. 1–5.

175 A. Hashim, 'The Egyptian Military, Part Two: From Mubarak Onward,' *Middle East Policy*, Vol. 18(4) (Winter 2011).

176 UNWC, supra note 65, Art. 3(5). Although the Convention was not in force, the principle of good faith is regarded as a general principle of law and perhaps as customary international law. See *Hungary v Slovakia*, supra note 55, Separate Opinion of Judge Bedjaoui, para. 60.

177 1993 Framework Instrument, supra note 173, preamble.

178 Ibid., Arts. 1–3.

substantive and procedural provisions. The latter includes 'creating appropriate mechanisms'[179] for cooperation.

Article 4 of the Framework Instrument further spelt out the following:

> The two Parties agree that the issue of the use of the Nile waters shall be worked out in detail, through discussions by experts from both sides, on the basis of the rules and principles of international law.

This article appears to contain both procedural and substantive elements. The stipulation that the use of water is subject to detailed expert study appears to be a procedural commitment, which ties into the notions of cooperation, creating mechanisms through which the two countries and their experts will work together, and promoting Basin-level cooperation as reaffirmed under Article 8 of the Framework. Likewise, the substantive dimension of Article 4 broadly, but vaguely, refers to 'rules and principles of international law.' Varied interpretations of this phrase are possible: on the one hand, the rules codified in colonial treaties can be interpreted as relevant rules and 'principles'; on the other hand, as discussed above, customary international watercourses law advocates, *inter alia*, the principle of equitable and reasonable utilization and participation, rather than a monopoly of use and decision making.

Article 5 of the Framework Instrument endorses the duty 'to refrain from engaging in any activity related to the Nile waters that may cause appreciable harm to the interests of the other party.' Oddly, while the customary international law umbrella principle of equitable use and participation[180] is absent from the Instrument, this subordinate rule to the principles is included. It should be noted that Article 7(1) of the UNWC refers to the duty to 'take all appropriate measures to prevent the causing of significant harm to other watercourse States' rather than 'to refrain from engaging in any activities.,' Arguably this makes the phrasing in the 1993 Framework Instrument more prohibitive and restrictive, especially when read in the light of the deliberate or unintended omission of the customary international law principle of equitable and reasonable use from the text. Yet, conserving and protecting Nile waters with the aim of enhancing the 'volume of flow and reduce the loss of Nile waters through comprehensive and integrated development schemes' was incorporated under Article 6 of the Framework Instrument.

179 Ibid., Arts. 4 & 7.

180 S. Salman, *The World Bank Policy for Projects on International Waterways: An Historical and Legal Analysis* (Washington, DC: The World Bank, 2009), pp. 95–96.

The Framework Instrument was hailed by some as "the nascent regime change in the Nile Basin,'[181] which helped in 'moving them more recently toward more cooperative behaviour.'[182] Given the history of rigid water sharing claims in the Basin, this observation is not without merit. However, it is doubtful, following the adoption of this instrument, that Egypt was committed to abandoning its historic 'right' claims, or that Ethiopia abandoned its equitable use claims.

The 1993 Framework Instrument is a written commitment signed by two heads of state, which might fulfil the definition of a treaty under Article 2(1)(a) of the VCLT. It was also later registered with the UN Secretariat.[183] To Mohamod Abdo,[184] the agreement

> merely represents the first attempt by the two states to come together, and does not have a binding effect. It is no more than the heralding of a new era of improved relations between the two states with regard to the water of the Nile.[185]

Shetewy, in contrast, concluded that 'Ethiopia had ratified' the agreement and 'pledged not to violate Egypt's historical rights.'[186] It is not clear whether the word 'ratified' was used here by Shetewy in its technical and legal sense, but a president cannot ratify a treaty under the Ethiopian Constitution.

As per Article 14 of the VCLT, the binding nature of such 'less formal agreements' depends on the intention of the parties to be bound by them under international law.[187] The ICJ applies an 'objective test' to determine whether a document gives rise to legal rights and duties under international law, taking into account 'its actual terms and ... the particular circumstances in which it

---

181 J. Brunnée & S. J. Toope, 'The Changing Nile Basin Regime: Does Law Matter?,' *Harvard International Law Journal*, Vol. 43(1) (2002), pp. 105–159, pp. 108–109.

182 Ibid., p. 110.

183 Framework Agreement, supra note 173, retrieved from https://treaties.un.org/Pages/showDetails.aspx?objid=0800000280 2a6733.

184 M. Abdo, 'The Nile Question: The Accords on the Water of the Nile and Their Implications on Cooperative Schemes in the Basin,' *Perceptions–Journal of International Affairs*, Vol. 9(2) (Summer 2004), pp. 45–57, retrieved from http://sam.gov.tr/wp-content/uploads/2012/01/4.-Mohammed-Abdo.pdf.

185 Ibid., p. 51.

186 Shetewy, *supra* note 124, p. 35.

187 J. Crawford, *Brownlie's Principles of Public International Law, 8th ed.* (Oxford: Oxford University Press, 2012), pp. 372–373.

was drawn up.'[188] In the present case, the formulation of intent on both sides cannot be deduced from the text and thus to support or reject either Shetewy's or Abdo's arguments. However, Abdo's argument makes sense in that, unlike the 2015 DoPs, the commitment in the Framework Instrument lacks specific rights and duties, including references to dispute resolution.

Nonetheless, the Instrument was registered with the UN in 2010,[189] in accordance with Article 102(1) of the UN Charter, which states that 'every treaty and every international agreement entered into by any Member of the United Nations ... shall *as soon as possible* be registered with the Secretariat and published by it.'[190] Unlike the League of Nations Covenant,[191] however, non-registration of an agreement does not determine its binding or non-binding nature.[192] The ICJ and other UN organs do not consider registration of an instrument when dealing with legal cases involving agreements concluded between states.[193] It follows that the UN Secretariat generally registers an agreement when it is submitted by any of the parties without making a judgement on the nature of that instrument.[194] In light of this, the registration of the 1993 Instrument by the UN upon Egypt's request suggests two viewpoints. On the one hand, Egypt meant it to be a binding commitment. The fact that it was relied upon to oppose the GERD reinforces this position.[195] On the other hand, Ethiopia neither backed (nor opposed) its registration with the UN, nor has it ratified it before its parliament. The move to register the instrument by Egypt after the lapse of 17 years arguably poses questions of good faith and might not be in compliance with the 'as soon as possible' precondition of Article 102(1) of the Charter. Even if it was registered in good faith, there was no shared understanding between the parties on the legal character of the instrument.

Assuming that the Framework Instrument is binding, it is highly unlikely that it gives rise to specific legal duties and entitlements[196] as it was broadly constructed and has not been supported by follow-up commitments. Again, if one concludes that the Instrument creates legal obligations, it follows that both

---

188 *Aegean Sea Continental Shelf Case (Greece v Turkey)*, [1978] ICJ Reports 3, para. 39.

189 1993 Framework Agreement, supra note 173.

190 Italics added.

191 The Covenant of the League of Nations, 28 April 1919, Art. 18.

192 Charter of the United Nations, 24 October 1945, Art. 102(2).

193 E. Martens, 'Article 102,' *in*, B. Simma et al, *The Charter of the United Nations: A Commentary, 3rd ed., Volume* 2, pp. 2098–2109 (Oxford: Oxford University Press, 2012), p. 2109.

194 Ibid.

195 Egypt's Perspective, supra 'note 5.

196 D. B. Hollis, *The Oxford Guide to Treaties Edited by Bibliographic Information* (Oxford: Oxford University Press, 2012), p. 32.

sides might have violated it, as is discussed further below. It should be noted that framework agreements must not be confused with framework conventions such as the United Nations Framework Convention on Climate Change. These are legally binding instruments,[197] whereas framework agreements do not normally require formal ratification,[198] the binding nature of which can only be determined on a case-by-case basis.

The 1993 Framework Instrument, different from what some had hoped for, is an unfinished and vague law-making endeavour, which has been selectively relied upon by the parties to blame each other for making use of Nile waters. Despite the ambiguity over its hard or soft law nature, it is an important commitment and part of a law-making process.[199] It has endorsed general principles, aspirations and a positive spirit of cooperation, which arguably and fundamentally differs from colonial-era Nile treaties and thus its impact on assessing the fairness of the GERD. This assertion requires further consideration but prior to doing so, the 2015 DoPs will be considered in order to engage in a discussion on the fairness or otherwise of these two post-1990 instruments more generally and with the most current one specifically.

The Declaration of Principles 2015

The DoPs, in contrast to the 1993 Framework Instrument, is a tripartite commitment signed by Egypt, Ethiopia and Sudan on 5 March 2015. It provides a relatively detailed insight into the opportunities and challenges of sharing water resources in the Eastern Nile Basin.[200] The interest here is to look into the connotations of the instrument to the fairness of the GERD. The general and specific principles on which the Declaration is founded are briefly reviewed first to help understand the fairness analysis.

---

197 K. Hossain, 'The Environmental Law-Making Process,' *in*, S. Alam et al, *Routledge Handbook of International Environmental Law*, pp. 61–76 (Abingdon: Routledge, 2013), p. 70. Arguably, however, the 'adoption, application, modification, interpretation and termination of treaties are, in principle, applicable to framework agreements and their protocols' as per N. Matz-Lück, 'Framework Conventions as a Regulatory Tool,' *Goettingen Journal of International Law*, Vol. 1(3) (2009), pp. 439–458, p. 442. It ought to be noted that the author appears to use the phrase 'framework convention' as synonymous to a 'framework agreement.'

198 G. Ulfstein, 'Reweaving the Fabric of International Law? Patters of Consent in Environmental Framework Agreements,' *in*, R. Wolfrum & V. Roben (eds.), *Developments of International Law in Treaty Making*, pp. 145–154 (Heidelberg: Springer, 2005), pp. 145–148.

199 Boyle & Chinkin, supra note 169, pp. 211–214; G. J. H. Van Hoof, *Rethinking the Sources of International Law* (Berlin: Kluwer, 1983), pp. 187–189.

200 Salman, supra note 15.

The DoPs aspires to promote the 'common interest' of, and cooperation among, the signatories, based on, *inter alia*, 'sovereign equality,' 'principles of international law,' 'good faith,' 'optimal use' and 'protection of the river.'[201] The 'Principle of Development, Regional Integration and Sustainability' further states:

> The purpose of GERD is for power generation, to contribute to economic development, promotion of transboundary cooperation and regional integration through generation of sustainable and reliable clean energy supply.[202]

This is reinforced by the principles of equitable use and no significant harm as enshrined in Articles III and IV respectively. The content of both principles is almost identical with the UNWC and the CFA notwithstanding some differences in the factors that are required to apply the equitable use principle. While the aspirations and some of the principles are found in the 1993 Framework Instrument, the DoPs not only recognizes a mega dam by a Nile upstream country, but also endorses fundamental principles of international watercourses law.[203]

The general principles are followed by a series of specific principles and practical commitments among which is the principle of dam safety,[204] which aims to prevent significant harm on Sudan and Egypt, the distinct standing of which (from the no-significant harm rule) is debatable. While the Berlin Rules on Water Resources[205] and some domestic legislation[206] regard dam safety as a normative rule, the Helsinki Rules, and most importantly the UNWC, do not explicitly mention dam safety. The World Commission on Dams, while stressing that building dams is a sovereign matter, recommend that dam building be handled within existing principles and rules of international watercourses law, including the principles of equitable use, no significant harm, good faith negotiations, and cooperation and with the use of an expert panel for

---

201 DoPs, supra note 12, Arts. I, IX.

202 Ibid., Art. II.

203 Ibid., Arts III, IV.

204 Ibid., Art. VIII.

205 Arts. 32 & 34.

206 See, e.g., Act to amend the National Dam Safety Program Act to reauthorize the national dam safety program, and for other purposes, 22 December 2006, Public Law 109–460 [USA], retrieved from https://www.congress.gov/109/plaws/publ460/PLAW-109publ460.pdf; National Water Act, 6 August 1998, Act No. 36 [South Africa], c. 12, retrieved from http://www.acts.co.za/national-water-act-1998/.

addressing concerns as required.[207] Based on these principles and consideration of whether or not dam safety is a (distinct) legal, as opposed to a policy, principle of international watercourses law, there is no doubt that it is a crucial part of the due diligence or the duty to take measures to prevent significant harm.

If an emergency[208] arises relating to a dam in a shared watercourse, as per Article 28(3) of the UNWC,

> [a] watercourse State within whose territory an emergency originates shall, in cooperation with potentially affected States and, where appropriate, competent international organisations, immediately take all practicable measures necessitated by the circumstances to prevent, mitigate and eliminate harmful effects of the emergency.

This appears to reiterate the duties enshrined in Article 7(2) of the UNWC concerning when significant harm has been caused, as considered above. Natural or man-made emergencies cause, or are most likely to cause, significant harm if they occur; it is therefore reasonable to expect swift action to prevent a human, socio-economic or natural disaster.

The DoPs has also adopted is 'the 'Principle to Cooperate on the First Filling and Operation of the Dam.'[209] This is accompanied by institutional and implementation mechanisms which include the establishment and use of national, joint and international bodies such as the IPoE and consultancy firms. Such technical and institutional mechanisms are vital to effective cooperation in matters concerning transboundary rivers.[210] Information and data exchange has also been considered as a principle that ought to be honoured 'in good faith and in a timely manner.'[211] However, the principle of confidence building

---

207 S. Salman, 'Dams, International Rivers, and Riparian States: An Analysis of the Recommendations of the World Commission on Dams,' *American University International Law Review*, Vol. 16(6) (2001), pp. 1477–1505. See pp. 1487–1503. For further discussion on human health and safety issues in the context of the primacy of the rule of significant harm, see Dellapenna, supra note 76, p. 283.

208 As per the UNWC (supra note 65), Article 28(1), 'emergency' means 'a situation that causes or poses an imminent threat of causing, serious harm to watercourse States or other States and that results suddenly from natural causes, such as floods, the breaking up of ice, landslides or earthquakes, or from human conduct, such as industrial accidents.'

209 DoPs, supra note 12, Art. V.

210 McCaffrey, supra note 73, p. 511.

211 DoPs, supra note 12, Art. VII.

through electric power sharing, with priority of power supply being given to Sudan and Egypt,[212] appears to be alien to the UNWC, the Helsinki and Berlin Rules, and the CFA, but not necessarily to transboundary water management frameworks.[213]

Before looking at the principles enshrined in the DoPs in terms of fairness, the following general points recap what has been considered thus far. First, the DoPs is founded on current legal thinking in the field to a greater extent than the 1993 Framework Instrument, which makes it distinct from old Nile treaties.[214] These current principles are translated into detailed commitments of cooperation, including on dam safety, filling and operation, and energy/benefit sharing. Finally, these principles appear to have been formulated in such a way to apply to the entire Nile as far as the use of Nile waters within respective territories of the parties is concerned. However, the legal status of the DoPs is unclear.

The binding nature of the DoPs depends on the content, wording and the intention of the parties.[215] Generally, it is a question of whether a written declaration made by two or more states 'generate[s] a normative *commitment*—a shared expectation of future behaviour whether in terms of a change from the *status quo* or a continuation of existing behaviour.'[216] Even if a declaration does not constitute a binding treaty, it can reaffirm established principles and customary rules of international law and thus be declaratory of legal duties and rights of states. Examples of such instruments include the Universal Declaration on Human Rights 1948[217] and the Declaration on the Friendly Relations between States 1970,[218] both of which are widely regarded

212 Ibid., Art. VI.

213 J. A. Allan & N. Mirumachi, 'Why Negotiate? Asymmetric Endowments, Asymmetric Power and the Invisible Nexus of Water, Trade and Power That Bring Apparent Water Security,' *in*, A. Earle, A. Jägerskog & J. Őjendal, *Transboundary Water Management: Principles and Practice*, pp. 13–26 (London: Earthscan, 2010), p. 22.

214 DoPs, *supra* note 12.

215 Ibid.

216 Hollis, supra note 196, p. 20.

217 Universal Declaration on Human Rights, 10 December 1948, Resolution 217 A(III), United Nations General Assembly.

218 Declaration on Principles of International Law concerning Friendly Relations and Co-operation among States in accordance with the Charter of the United Nations, 24 October 1970, Resolution 2625 (XXV), United Nations General Assembly.

as authoritative sources or an affirmation of existing law.[219] Similarly, bilateral or trilateral declarations may be legally binding, depending on their details and circumstances of conclusion.[220] The ICJ in the 2002 *Cameroon/Nigeria*[221] boundary delimitation case endorsed a declaration as a legal instrument despite some technical shortcomings.[222]

Three arguments can be considered with respect to the legal character of the GERD's DoPs. The first argument would be that the DoPs, similar, if not identical, to the 1993 Framework Instrument, is a soft law (which is not binding) rather than a hard law (which is legally binding) instrument. The absence of formal phrases including a clause on entry into force, ratification and deposit as stipulated in Article 24 (4) of the VCLT can be cited as evidence to support this. The Ethiopian Parliament has not ratified the Declaration, which is similar to their practice with the 1993Framework Instrument. Neither the Egyptian House of Representatives[223] nor the Sudanese National Legislature[224] have approved the DoPs as required by both states' constitutions. Importantly, the Egyptian Constitution 2014[225] maintains 'Egypt's [Nile] historic rights,' which appears to be in conflict with the principles enshrined in the DoPs. Further,

219 *Case Concerning Military and Paramilitary Activities in and Against Nicaragua (Nicaragua v United States of America)*, Judgement of 27 June 1986 (Merits), [1986] ICJ Reports 14, paras. 187–201.

220 *Case Concerning Maritime Delimitation and Territorial Questions Between Qatar And Bahrain (Qatar v Bahrain)*, Judgement of 1 July 1994 (Jurisdiction and Admissibility), [1994] ICJ Reports 112.

221 The Court concluded that 'the boundary between the Republic of Cameroon and the Federal Republic of Nigeria in the Lake Chad area is delimited by the Thomson-Marchand *Declaration* of 1929–1930, as incorporated in the Henderson-Fleuriau Exchange of Notes of 1931' (italics added) (*Case Concerning the Land and Maritime Boundary Between Cameroon and Nigeria (Cameroon v Nigeria: Equatorial Guinea intervening)*, [2002] ICJ Reports 303, para. 325(1)[A], p. 454.

222 Ibid.

223 Egyptian Constitution, supra note 6. Article 151 reads:

> The President of the Republic shall represent the State in its foreign relations and conclude treaties and ratify them after the approval of the House of Representatives. Such treaties shall acquire the force of law following their publication in accordance with the provisions of the Constitution.

224 Interim National Constitution of the Republic of Sudan, 6 July' 2005, Art. 58(1)(k).

225 The Constitutional provision states: 'The state commits to protecting the Nile River, maintaining Egypt's historic rights thereto, rationalizing and maximizing its benefits, not wasting its water or polluting it…' (Egyptian Constitution, supra note 6).

Egypt and Sudan have not formally denounced Nile colonial-era treaties[226] or justified their compatibility with the DoPs. Certain colonial-era treaties[227] appear to be in conflict with the DoPs, in particular, the equitable utilisation principle.[228] These are among the indications and circumstances that suggest that the parties did not mean the DoPs to be a normative commitment.

In contrast, the second argument would be that the DoPs is a hard law agreement, which must be honoured in 'good faith.'[229] Such legal agreements do not necessarily need to be ratified by parliament to have international legal effect as ascertaining the intention to be bound by a treaty is determined and 'governed by international law.'[230] In the DoPs case, the intention of the parties can be inferred from the document itself. At the outset, the title of the instrument refers to 'agreement,' which is different from the 1993 Framework Instrument. The Declaration not only sets out or reaffirms existing legal principles that are adopted in conventional and customary international law but also specific commitments, some with immediate effect. This was one of the reasons why the ICJ ruled in support of Bahrain's argument that minutes of a meeting constituted a binding agreement.[231] It is established in international law that 'a state may not invoke the provisions of its internal law as justifications for its failure to perform a treaty.'[232] Clearly, Ethiopia, Sudan and Egypt cannot rely on their respective constitutions to not honour their commitments in the DoPs.

The reference to 'dispute settlement' and 'interpretation' of the Declaration in accordance with 'the principle of good faith' (which borrows the language of Article 26 of VCLT) is further evidence that the parties meant to create legal

226 A. Aman, 'Egypt Warily Signs Preliminary Nile Agreement,' *Al-monitor* (31 March 2015), retrieved from http://www.al-monitor.com/pulse/originals/2015/03/egypt-eastern-nile-water-agreement-ethiopia-sudan.html#.

227 As discussed above under 'Colonial Treaties and the Fairness of the GERD' and below under 'Concluding Remarks.'

228 H. Hammam, *A Legal Analysis of the Declaration of Principles on the Grand Ethiopian Renaissance Dam*, Public International Law Blog, retrieved from https://law4371.wordpress.com/2015/05/08/a-legal-analysis-of-the-declaration-of-principles-on-the-grand-ethiopian-renaissance-dam/

229 *Cameroon v Nigeria*, supra note 221, para. 39; VCLT, supra note 139, Art. 26.

230 Waldoc, Sir H., 'First Report on the Law of Treaties,' *in*, *Yearbook of the International Law Commission 1962, Vol. II*, pp. 27–80 (New York: United Nations, 1964), p. 32, retrieved from http://legal.un.org/ilc/publications/yearbooks/english/ilc_1962_v2.pdf.

231 *Qatar v Bahrain*, supra note 220.

232 VCLT, supra note 139, Art. 27; *Legal Status of Eastern Greenland*, PCIJ Series A/B No 53 (5 April 1933), paras. 5–18.

rights and duties, although judicial and arbitral methods are not referred to in the instrument. What methods of dispute settlement states adopt is a matter for states to decide, which is why the selective approach taken by the DoPs may not show an intention not to be bound by the DoPs as a matter of law. Finally, the wording 'shall' rather than 'would' or 'will' in relation to the core principles enshrined in Articles III (not inflicting significant harm), IV (equitable principle) and VII (data exchange), amongst others, is sound textual evidence of the intention to be bound by the terms and commitments. Unless this was caused by a bad drafting of the text, or a poor translation from the original languages, from Arabic to English,[233] these terms appear to connote that the DoPs is a hard law instrument.

These assertions may well be challenged by the fact that the two downstream countries believe in the application of Nile colonial treaties that are not formally renounced (or upheld) in the DoPs. However, a state does not need to officially denounce prior legal commitments in order to endorse or reject a subsequent legal commitment as past treaties can be put aside or abrogated through the adoption of subsequent legal commitments on the same subject matter.[234] Such an abrogation of old Nile treaties based on the doctrine of *lex priori* can be justified and necessary for progressive development of the law.[235]

The third argument avoids, but also supplements, these two extreme views and submits that, whether hard or soft law, the DoPs is declaratory and an endorsement of modern principles and rules of existing customary international law, and those principles and rules, as reflected in the DoPs, would be binding upon the parties. Even if the DoPs itself is not legally binding upon the parties, the official endorsement of principles and rules of international law (by Egypt and Sudan in particular) can be seen as evidence of an emerging consensus in the Eastern Nile Basin to make an initial deal on the GERD and any other similar project based on contemporary international law.

The question of implementing or disregarding the DoPs and associated undertakings as consensual commitments is a difficult one to deal with. One possible answer is that the commitments are not implemented and respected as the anticipated studies to be carried out by the French firm are delayed while

233 See, e.g., the Arabic to English translation of the DoPs by Ahramonline, retrieved from http://english.ahram.org.eg/News/125941.aspx.

234 VCLT, *supra* note 139, Art. 59(1)(b).

235 J. Klabbers, 'Beyond the Vienna Convention: Conflicting Treaty Provisions,' *in*, E. Cannizzaro (ed.), *The Law of Treaties Beyond the Vienna Convention*, pp. 192–205 (Oxford: Oxford University Press, 2011), p. 197.

construction of the dam is ongoing.[236] The other possible answer is that the parties to the DoPs are implementing and reaffirming their commitments. It could be argued that the delays caused by technical and administrative challenges that the three countries and the firms have been facing do not necessarily mean they are disregarding their commitments. For instance, the DoPs itself acknowledges that 'the Three Countries appreciate the efforts undertaken thus far by Ethiopia in implementing the IPoE recommendations pertinent to the GERD["s] safety.'[237] This endorsement is important because the DoPs refers to the need to implement the recommendations of the IPoE. Furthermore, the three countries adopted the December 2015 Khartoum minutes, reaffirming their commitments to the DoPs, which led to (a) the selection of two French firms to conduct the required studies and a British law firm to administer the contract between the parties; (b) the adoption of an annex that contains the 'roadmap and plans for the studies'; and (c) an agreement that a regular meeting at the ministerial level continues to expedite the process.[238] Most importantly, Article 5 of the Khartoum minutes

> dealt with confidence-building and stated that the three countries agree to support and encourage efforts aimed at promoting confidence-building measures so as to enhance people-to-people relations of the three countries. Accordingly, Ethiopia invited parliamentarians, the media, and public diplomacy groups of both Egypt and Sudan to visit the GERD.[239]

In September 2016, these developments were followed by the signing of a contract between the three countries and BRLi Group and Artelia regarding the studies to be carried out on the impacts and hydrology of the GERD.[240] According to an Egyptian newspaper, *Ahramonline*, the meeting that led to the signing of the contract

---

236 See, 'Ethiopia Won't Stop Construction of the Renaissance Dam: Minister,' *Sudan Tribune* (13 February 2016), retrieved from http://www.sudantribune.com/spip.php?article57997.

237 DoPs, supranote 12, Art. VIII. For the Panel's final report, see '*International Panel of Experts (IPoE) on Grand Ethiopian Renaissance Dam Project (GERDP) Final Report*,' (31 May 2013), retrieved from https://www.internationalrivers.org/sites/default/files/attached-files/international_panel_of_experts_for_ethiopian_renaissance_dam-_final_report_1.pdf [IPoE Report].

238 Salman, supra note 15, p. 524.

239 Ibid.

240 See, 'Egypt, Ethiopia, Sudan Sign,' supra note 18'.

> was conducted in a very friendly and warm environment and reflected the cooperation among the three countries and all in attendance expressed their support and appreciation for the efforts exerted by the three countries.[241]

However, whether the impact studies to be carried by the two French firms will arrive before or after the completion of the GERD remains to be seen. It is most likely that two turbines (out of 16) will commence generating electricity before the completion of the studies/reports. Even if the reports will not be used for or help with the actual construction of the dam, they may still be valuable for dealing with reservoir filling[242] and operation of the dam.

From an Egyptian (and possibly Sudanese) perspective, it might be argued that the continued construction of the GERD' without considering the outcomes of the forthcoming studies disregards Ethiopia's commitment to the DoPs. From the Ethiopian perspective, however, this assumption has several defects. First, the conclusions in the studies may or may not have any implications for the way in which Salini is constructing the GERD. Second, demanding a halt to construction because of technical and administrative hurdles will be very costly to Ethiopia. Third, the delay in commencing the studies cannot be attributed to Ethiopia alone—all the parties, including the private firms, contributed to the delay[243] in one way or another. Fourth, there is no evidence that the DoPs was agreed to in the spirit that the construction of the dam was conditional upon the studies contemplated under it (the ICJ, in the *Pulp Mills* case, specifically pronounced the position of the law on this stating that suspension of the Pulp Mills project was only possible 'in conformity with the provisions of the treaty' or 'by consent of all the parties')[244] and, finally, as the Dams Commission hints, it may not be equitable and reasonable to halt the GERD project simply because there is a delay in forthcoming studies by foreign firms that are not of binding character. Some of these issues will be revisited when the DoPs' connotations to the fairness principle are considered below.

The parties to the DoPs have not only come up with solid agreement on principles, but they are also implementing, or trying to implement, the commitments adopted in the DoPs, although the process does not appear to be going smoothly. Regardless of the validity of the various scenarios on the legal

241 Ibid.

242 Salman, supra note 15, p. 524.

243 See, e.g., 'Egypt Announces Postponement of GERD Impact Studies Contracts Signing,' *Ahramonline* (4 September 2016), retrieved from http://english.ahram.org.eg/News/242347.aspx.

244 *Pulp Mills, supra* note 46, para. 141.

status of the instrument, the DoPs evidences the beginning, not the end, of a new era—whether that era is that of fairness or *status quo ante* depends on the appreciation and interpretation of the commitments made in the instrument.

GERD's Fairness in the Context of Post-1990 Commitments

This section tackles the issues of the fairness of damming the Blue Nile and its implications for cooperation from the perspective of non-colonial-era commitments. While the DoPs offers solid perspectives on the distributive justice aspect of fairness, the 1993 Framework Instrument poses more procedural questions.

GERD's Procedural Fairness

The 1993 Framework Instrument was among the grounds relied upon to either challenge or justify the procedural fairness of the GERD. Shetewy, for example, impliedly argues against the construction of the GERD on the grounds that Ethiopia, as well as Egypt, has, in the 1993 Instrument, pledged to conduct consultations and establish joint mechanisms and studies for using Nile waters.[245] Accordingly, Ethiopia has 'failed' to comply with these pledges and therefore infringed procedural fairness. From an Egyptian perspective, Ethiopia did not comply with the procedural duty of prior notification and consultation concerning technical data and potential impacts of the GERD before commencing construction. This is particularly true if it was thought that the project may have a significant adverse effect on the downstream states.[246] As a matter of law, Ethiopia only has to notify if its planned project 'may have a significant adverse effect upon other watercourse States,' as expressly enshrined in Article 12 of the UNWC. Although the duty to notify does not equate to the right to veto a planned project, the duty to notify has attained general principle or customary law status in the field of watercourses law.[247]

Given that the duty to notify is procedural, however, it is normally and primarily applied within a treaty framework.[248] Most importantly, in situations

---

245 Shetewy, supra note 124, p. 35.

246 UNWC, supra note 65, Arts. 11–12; Shetewy, supra note 124, pp. 30–31.

247 P. Wouters, *International Water Law: Selected Writings of Professor Charles B. Bourne* (Leiden: Martinus Nijhoff, 1997), p. 182. The ICJ in the *Pulp Mills* case (supra note 46) states that 'the obligation to inform CARU [Adminstrative Commission of the River Uruguay, a body established by a treaty] allows for the initiation of co-operation between the Parties which is necessary in order to fulfil the obligation of prevention' (para. 102).

248 See, *Pulp Mills*, supra note 46, paras. 112–122, in particular para. 122. In this case, the 1975 Statute (a treaty) signed by both countries enshrined, *inter alia*, 'the obligation of prior notification.' The Court adopted the same approach in *Dispute Regarding Navigational*

where two or more basin states are not parties to relevant international, basin-level or bilateral agreements that oblige them to notify other states on planned projects, and non-notification is the norm rather than the exception in relations among co-riparians,[249] the application of the principles of reciprocity and equity ought not be ignored.[250] As the Permanent Court of International Justice (PCIJ) put it:

> It would seem to be an important principle of equity that where two parties have assumed an identical or a reciprocal obligation, one party which is engaged in a continuing non-performance of that obligation should not be permitted to take advantage of a similar non-performance of that obligation by the other party.[251]

In this respect, what Egypt had demanded was what it has never given to Ethiopia and other upstream countries. The proposal to build the Aswan High Dam (AHD) was not shared with Ethiopia. Most significantly, Egypt never consulted with or shared the benefits of the South Valley Toshka Project (or the Al Salam Canal which diverts the Nile to Sinai) with upstream countries.[252] The Aswan Dam is only of historical significance here. The South Valley/Toshka scheme, in contrast, began in 1997, after the signing of the 1993 Framework Instrument, and was meant to expand Egypt's irrigated land by 'up to 3,200 sq km' and have the capacity to support around six million Egyptians.[253] This is a new and ongoing development that reinforces the prior apportionment claim by Egypt over Nile waters, which requires an additional 5 to 10 billion cubic metres of Nile waters.[254] Without going into the polemics of the impact

---

and Related Rights (*Costa Rica v Nicaragua*), Judgement of 13 July 2009, [2009] ICJ Reports 213, paras. 91–97.

249 Salman, supra note 92, p. 22.

250 *Diversion of Water*, supra note 59, para. 323.

251 Ibid.

252 Z. A. Yigzaw, *Open Letter to Egypt: A Response to The Spokesman of Egypt's Ministry of Foreign Affairs Regarding the GERDP from An Ethiopian Perspective*, Abbay Nile (28 March 2014), retrieved from https://zenileabbay.wordpress.com/2014/03/28/open-letter-to-egypt-a-response-to-the-spokes-man-of-egypts-ministry-of-foreign-affairs-regarding-gerdp-from-an-ethiopian-perspective/.

253 N. Wahish, 'Toshka Turns Millennial Green,' *Al-Ahram Weekly On-line*, Issue No. 392 (27 August–2 September 1998), retrieved from http://weekly.ahram.org.eg/archive/1998/392/ec1.htm.

254 Woldetsadik, supra note 128, pp. 44–45; A. E. Cascão, 'Changing Power Relations in the Nile River Basin: Unilateralism vs. Cooperation?,' Water Alternatives, Vol. 2(2) (2009), pp. 245–268, p. 249.

of this project on the Nile River system, the actions that occurred before and after the 1993 Framework Instrument speak for themselves concerning the unjustifiability of Egypt's attempt to object to the GERD on the basis of not being notified and consulted with during planning.

The duty to notify and consult is seen as customary law,[255] hence of an *erga omnes* character owed to all Nile Basin countries; its violation by Egypt with respect to the Aswan Dam or its most recent project does not justify Ethiopia's 'failure' to notify and consult with Egypt. The problem of such a noble but 'rigid' application of a procedural rule without sufficient account of practices and behaviours of riparian states in a particular river basin would be contrary to what the PCIJ termed the principles of reciprocity and equity, which require equal treatment and the expectation that all basin states apply legal rules and principles.[256] Furthermore, if a riparian state invokes a violation of a procedural rule of international law by another co-riparian state, whilst itself is engaged in violating the same rule, that conduct may amount to an abuse of rights and processes[257] and thus be considered unjust. This conclusion is further strengthened by the fact that Ethiopia strongly believes in the absence of a significant risk of harm to downstream countries as a result of its dam project.

It is doubtful that the doctrine of abuse of rights or processes exists in international law,[258] and thus the rule of prior notification or consultation, as enshrined in Article 11 of the UNWC, ought to be adhered to strictly, disregarding the peculiar complexities of the practices and contentions over shared Nile waters. If this line of argument holds true, both Egypt and Ethiopia would be responsible for not honouring their respective commitment not to engage in planned Nile projects without a joint study and prior notification and consultation, as can be broadly inferred from the 1993 Framework Instrument, notwithstanding the controversy surrounding the binding nature of the Instrument. Furthermore, as the ICJ in the *Pulp Mills* case affirmed, it is every state's duty 'not to allow knowingly its territory to be used for acts contrary to the rights of other States.'[259] It follows from this that 'a State is ... obliged to use all the means at its disposal in order to avoid activities which take place in its territory,

255 A. Rieu-Clarke, 'Notification and Consultation on Planned Measures Concerning International Watercourses: Learning from the Pulp Mills and Kishenganga Cases,' *Yearbook of International Environmental Law*, Vol. 24(1) (2014), pp. 102–130.

256 *Diversion of Water*, *supra* note 59; CFA, supra note 94, Art. 10.

257 H. Lauterpacht, *The Function of Law in the International Community* (Oxford: Oxford University Press, 2011), pp. 306–307.

258 Wouters, *supra* note 247, p. 76.

259 *Pulp Mills*, supra note 46, para. 101.

or in any area under its jurisdiction, causing significant damage to the environment of another State.'[260] This is termed by the Court as the duty of prevention, the implementation of which is reliant on cooperation between the concerned parties. The duty to inform/notify 'allows for the initiation of (such) co-operation.'[261] This due diligence expectation may therefore apply to both Ethiopia and Egypt.

Egypt may also be found responsible for breaking the 1993 Framework Instrument as statements made during the Morsi era and in earlier reports indicate the plans and 'determination' of Egypt to use military force, or threat of force, subversion and the like, to halt construction of the GERD';[262] these actions may have contravened 'the principles of good neighbourliness, peaceful settlement of disputes, and non-interference in the internal affairs of states.'[263] Such Egyptian conduct also defeats the core of UN Charter and AU commitments that deploying, or threatening to deploy, military force to promote economic or other interests of a state is firmly prohibited in contemporary international law.[264] In particular it was/is not clear whether the threatening statements made by Egyptian politicians were mere political rhetoric or steps taken as part of a concrete and planned state action.[265] In recent months, however, 'Ethiopia has accused Egypt and Eritrea of destabilizing its stability by supporting outlawed rebels and stoking an unprecedented wave of protests that has led the government to declare a six-month state of emergency,'[266] an allegation that was swiftly denied by Egypt.[267]

Such accusations and counter-accusations on past and recent events are unlikely to promote genuine cooperation among the parties, which is the prime objective of a fair process. In part, therefore, this discussion may be academic and obsolete. Furthermore, the 1993 Framework Instrument offers more than the two main issues discussed thus far, the general ban on the use of Nile waters and prior notification as procedural matters. For instance, both sides

---

260 Ibid.

261 Ibid., para. 102.

262 D. Whittington, J. Waterbury & M. Jeuland, 'The Grand Renaissance Dam and Prospects for Cooperation on the Eastern Nile,' *Water Policy*, Vol. 16(4) (2014), pp. 595–608, p. 598. DOI: 10.2166/wp.2014.011; Kelley & Johnson, supra note 11.

263 1993 Framework Instrument, supra note 173, Art. 1.

264 C. Gray, 'The Use of Force and the International Legal Order,' *in*, M. D. Evans (ed.), *International Law, 3rd ed.*, pp. 615–647 (Oxford: Oxford University Press, 2010), pp. 618–619.

265 Yihdego, supra note 170.

266 N. Ali, 'Ethiopia Accuses Egypt of Destabilizing the Country by Supporting Rebels,' *Middle East Observer* (11 October 2016).

267 See, 'Egypt's Sisi denies supporting opposition in Ethiopia,' *Reuters* (13 October 2016).

agreed to 'create appropriate mechanism[s] for periodic consultations'[268] and, most importantly, they committed themselves to work 'towards a framework for effective cooperation among countries of the Nile Bain.'[269] These are positive commitments which might have contributed to the endeavour made to establish the NBI and, ultimately, the CFA.

Undoubtedly, the DoPs has opened a new chapter of cooperation and provides comprehensive insight into the procedural fairness of the GERD. Before dealing with the fairness of the adoption and implementation processes of the DoPs, a background discussion on the design of the project is desirable to see to what extent GERD's initial processes were participatory for relevant stakeholders in accordance with internationally acceptable standards. The Dam's Commission rightly states:

> Large dams arise from a series of decisions taken from the beginning of the planning process through to the final approval of a project and financial closure. At each stage different actors are involved, including government agencies, public or private utilities, interested parties from the region, financing agencies, consulting and construction companies and equipment suppliers. Affected people and NGOs are increasingly involved as well.'[270]

The GERD appears to have secured the participation of most, if not all, these actors and their vital roles in the process of designing and planning the project. The following three points demonstrate this. First, building upon previous studies, the government conducted a series of studies, including dam design, environmental and socio-economic impact assessment, initial transboundary environmental impact assessment, and flood analysis.[271] The IPoE, it its 2013 report, confirmed, for example, that the content and structure of the environmental impact assessment conducted to identify the impacts of the GERD on Ethiopia, Sudan and Egypt met the standards of international financial institutions.[272] Similarly, the hydrological study on flood analysis was generally

268 1993 Framework Agreement, supra note 173, Art. 7.

269 Ibid., Art. 8.

270 See, World Commission on Dams, *Dams and Development—A New Framework for Decision-making* (London: Earthscan, 2000), p. 167.

271 IPoE Report, supra note 237, pp. 14–39.

272 Ibid., see in particular p. 28.

acceptable.[273] The Panel also made recommendations in relation to implementation of the project and the DoPs.

Second, the IPoE also said that the Geotechnical Mission Report[274] prepared by the contractor, Salini, was of an internationally acceptable quality. Salini is not the only European company that is involved in the GERD's design and implementation. Alstom, a French company, signed a contract worth 250 million Euro in 2013 with the state-owned Metals & Engineering Corporation (METEC) to supply all of the GERD turbines and other electrical equipment and to supervise their installation.[275] The Chinese have also been involved with the design and execution of building transmission lines from the GERD to the national grid.[276]

Third, the GERD was designed to be financed by the Ethiopian government and the public, which makes it a unique self-funded mega project, free from foreign loans or aid. The Ethiopian public both at home and abroad was made aware of the commencement of the project, including the modality of financing the project. As will be discussed below, despite some legitimate questions and doubts from some quarters, Ethiopians and foreign citizens of Ethiopian origin have rallied around financing and supporting the GERD project.[277] This includes those who are, or will be, displaced by the project.[278] Ethiopian local and international civil and professional societies firmly support(ed) the initiation of the GERD[279] while the U.S.-based non-governmental organization International Rivers opposed it from the outset.

The two downstream countries, Egypt and Sudan, did not participate in the design of the GERD. The procedural fairness of the initiation of the GERD might therefore be doubted. The unilateral nature of the dam project, which

273 Ibid., p. 34.

274 Ibid., p. 29.

275 Altsom, 'Alstom to Supply Hydroelectric Equipment for the Grand Renaissance Dam in Ethiopia,' Press Release (7 January 2013), retrieved from http://www.alstom.com/press-centre/2013/1/alstom-to-supply-hydroelectric-equipment-for-the-grand-renaissance-dam-in-ethiopia/.

276 Y. Tadele, 'EEPCo, Chinese Company Ink Billion Dollar Transmission Line Deal,' *Fortune*, Vol. 13(678) (28 April 2013).

277 See Office of National Council for the Coordination of Public Participation on The Grand Renaissance Dam, retrieved from http://www.hidasse.gov.et/.

278 J. Veilleux, 'The Human Security Dimensions of Dam Development: The Grand Ethiopian. Renaissance Dam,' *Global Dialogue*, Vol. 15(2) (2013), p. 10, retrieved from http://www.transboundarywaters.orst.edu/publications/publications/Veilleux_GLOBAL%20DIALOGUE_V15_GERD.pdf.

279 See, e.g., *Ethiopian International Professional Support for Abay*, Ethiopian International Professional Support for Abay/Nile (EIPSA), retrieved from http://www.eipsa1.com/cms/.

was initiated in the absence of any relevant treaty regime between the three countries, might justify the initial non-participation of the two key stakeholders. Although the GERD is much bigger than previous projects, Egypt and Sudan participated the planning and design of a dam that was intended to be built on the Blue Nile within the NBI framework.[280]Even if the procedural fairness of the beginning of the GERD is characterized by this likely 'weakness,' the three aforementioned points broadly affirm that the initial process was not only participatory but also founded on scientific studies and processes involving internationally (and nationally) recognized actors. Most importantly, fairness is a process, and might not begin as a perfect one. Furthermore, the two downstream countries were later 'invited in good faith ... to review the design documents of the GERD'[281] with the purpose of building trust and confidence among the three eastern Nile countries.

The adoption of the DoPs by the three countries seems to have rectified what was missing at the design level by making links between issues of design and other studies and implementation of the Declaration. The question is, however, was the adoption of the DoPs fair? A series of meetings by representatives of the three countries at the technical, ministerial and head of state/government levels[282] demonstrates equality, serious exchange of ideas and a spirit of cooperation. These negotiations provided the parties with opportunities to exchange their hopes and fears and also to make compromises, as can be shown from the DoPs itself. For example, Ethiopia agreed to use the GERD for energy generation purposes and to make the sale of electricity to Sudan and Egypt a priority, while the two downstream countries made an unprecedented move to endorse contemporary principles of international watercourses law. Arguably this is further evidence that the adoption of the DoPs is a result of a fair process. What is clear is that the legality of the construction of the GERD has become uncontentious. Indeed, the dam has been seen as an opportunity to foster development and integration.[283] This does not close the question of fair and legitimate adoption and participation, however.

It is contended that Ethiopia has forced Egypt (and not Sudan) to agree on the construction and operation of the dam as a *fait accompli*.[284] It appears

280 A. E. Cascão & A. Nicol, 'GERD: New Norms of Cooperation in the Nile Basin?,' *Water International*, Vol. 41(4) (2016), pp. 559–560.

281 IPoE Report, supra note 237, p. 1.

282 Salman, supra note 15.

283 DoPs, supra note 12, Art. II.

284 See, 'Egypt Forced to Negotiate on Nile Dam,' *Stratfor* (20 March 2015), retrieved from https://www.stratfor.com/sample/analysis/egypt-forced-negotiate-nile-dam; H. Verhoeven, 'Africa's Next Hegemon: Behind Ethiopia's Power Plays,' *Foreign Affairs* (12 April 2015),

from the terms of DoPs itself,[285] earlier statements made by Egyptian officials, and the major shift of its position that Egypt might have made an informed decision to support, or even to participate in jointly building, the GERD[286] as it is beneficial to its water, energy and other geo-political interests; this is of course conditional, amongst others, upon reaching an agreement on dam filling and operation policy.[287] To Sudan, in contrast, 'backing the dam project is not a political stance, but rather a belief in its benefits for all Nile Basin states.'[288] This belief of President Omar Al-Bashir is shared by scholars with specific reference to the benefits of the dam to Sudan.[289]

Ethiopia, for its part, as evidence of compliance with its due diligence duty to take 'all appropriate measures' to prevent harm,[290] went to the extent of inviting Egypt and Sudan to establish a Tripartite Joint Commission and an IPoE to follow up on the construction of the GERD and issues arising from its design, construction and operation, with the purpose of ensuring downstream participation in pre-and-post project completion policy and operational matters. This was also recommended by the IPoE.[291] However, despite undertaking internal and (initial) transboundary environmental (and social) impact assessments that were said to have met international funding agencies' standards, the IPoE recommended that further studies were needed to elaborate on some of the studies concerning downstream impacts.[292] Ethiopia agreed to strengthen its studies. Despite varied interpretations of the findings and recommendations of the IPoE report, the parties recognize Ethiopia's efforts to 'implement the IPoE recommendations'.[293] As considered above, the contract

---

retrieved from https://www.foreignaffairs.com/articles/ethiopia/2015-04-12/africas-next-hegemon; S. Farid, 'Will Egypt Still Get Its Fair Share of Nile Water?.' *Al Arabiya News* (31 March 2015), retrieved from http://english.alarabiya.net/en/perspective/analysis/2015/03/31/Will-Egypt-still-get-its-fair-share-of-Nile-water-.html.

285 DoPs, supra note 12, Art. II.

286 A. Aman, 'In Switch, Egypt May Join Ethiopia in Nile Dam Project,' *Al-monitor* (21 October 2013), retrieved from http://www.al-monitor.com/pulse/originals/2013/10/egypt-ethiopia-dam-reconciliation.html#ixzz4UK9hCjUq.

287 Ibid. There was also a demand to reduce the size of reservoir, which was rejected by Ethiopia.

288 Eleiba, supra note.

289 R. Tawfik, 'The Grand Ethiopian Renaissance Dam: A Benefit-sharing Project in the Eastern Nile?,' *Water International*, Vol. 41(4) (2016), pp. 574–592.

290 UNWC, supra note 65, Art. 7(1).

291 IPoE, supra note 237.

292 Ibid., pp. 39–40; see also *Pulp Mills, supra* note 46, paras. 203–219.

293 DoPs, supra note 12, Art. VIII.

between the three countries and the two French firms is intended to follow up the suggestions made by the IPoE.

The parties have now agreed 'to cooperate on the first filling and operation' of the GERD,[294] the details of which will be informed by the IPoE report, joint studies and decision of the three countries.[295] Joint technical national committees and a Committee of Water (and Foreign) Ministers are empowered to deal with this crucial task. The reference to the heads of state (or government) of the three countries as ultimate arbitrators in case a dispute arises is an important mechanism for fully and flexibly implementing the Declaration. The Dam's Commission Guidelines on dam related disputes refer, however, to 'good faith negotiations or independent dispute resolution procedures.'[296] Political methods of dispute settlement are certainly more flexible, swift and less costly when undertaken in good faith and a spirit of cooperation compared to legal or other independent methods of dispute settlement.

In brief, the DoPs secured consensus of the three eastern Nile Basin countries on the continuing construction of the GERD and the way in which it will be filled and operated and how the benefits will be shared—an exemplary practice in promoting procedural fairness in the use of shared water resources such as Nile waters. The project design and implementation have also involved various actors—government agencies, the three countries, contractors and suppliers, foreign consultancy firms, and communities—although this process has not been without shortcomings. Translating such key consensual commitments and processes into distributive justice is a necessary but difficult exercise, as the following section will show.

GERD's Distributive Justice

Some Key General Issues

In contrast to assessment of GERD's procedural fairness, which appears to have been put to rest in March 2015, evaluating the distributive justice impacts of GERD based upon the two post-1990 instruments is much more intricate. Undoubtedly, the 1993 Framework Instrument conveys, in incomplete terms, a message of distributive justice on the sharing of Nile resources, which may be used to support or question the fairness of the GERD. The Instrument includes

294 Ibid., Art. v.

295 Zhang et al, supra note 20; see also K. G. Wheeler et al, 'Cooperative Filling Approaches for the Grand Ethiopian Renaissance Dam,' *Water International*, Vol. 41(4) (2016), pp. 611–634.

296 World Commission of Dams, supra note 270, p. 267.

the commitment to cooperate on advancing 'economic and political interests' of both parties.[297] This must be read in conjunction with the term 'mutual interest,' which is repeatedly referred to as a foundation for their cooperation on Nile and other matters. Furthermore, conserving and protecting Nile waters by enhancing 'the volume of flow and reduc[ing] the loss of Nile waters'[298] constitutes one of its core commitments. The Instrument also reaffirms the prevention of causing 'appreciable harm.'[299] By endorsing the interests of both parties, these basic commitments broadly advance some of the requirements of distributive justice, which also take into account preserving Nile waters. However, the Instrument offers almost nothing with respect to substantive water use rights of the parties, and thus is not a complete instrument for fostering distributive justice.

Egypt relied on the appreciable harm clause, *inter alia*, of the 1993 Framework Instrument to argue that the GERD will be detrimental to its agriculture, fisheries, and hydropower and harm the natural environment.[300] If substantiated, this claim would make the GERD at odds with distributive justice. Ethiopia strongly contests these claims and sees the dam as beneficial in regulating flooding and slit, increasing Blue Nile flows and reducing evaporation loses from the Aswan Dam and other storage dams in Sudan, thus promoting some of the terms of the 1993 Instrument. All these assertions, including the clean energy generation and sharing, promote mutual interest and a 'win-win' situation among the parties, and thus promote justice rather than harm.[301] Different from the 1993 Instrument, however, the DoPs has adopted ten general and specific principles of international (watercourses) law that set out the fundamentals of a fair deal for all concerned, which is entirely different from old Nile treaties and practices. The DoPs, building upon the core principles, attempts to balance conflicting interests. Ethiopia's right to use the river for hydropower generation is firmly endorsed. In fact, the DoPs recognizes the dam as a catalyst for regional integration and sustainable development. However, it barred the dam from being used for irrigation purposes, which provides a 'symbolic' guarantee to Egypt and Sudan. In addition, Ethiopia has agreed to share the benefits of the GERD by giving priority of exporting electricity to Sudan and Egypt. By this account, the GERD's benefits will be shared by the

297 1993 Framework Agreement, supra note 173, Art. 3.

298 Ibid., Art 6.

299 Ibid., Art 5.

300 Egypt's Perspective, supra 'note 5.

301 Whittington et al, supra note 262, pp. 596 600; MIT Report, supra note 10.

three parties and other Nile riparian countries and thus appears to be in line with the notion of 'broadly conceived equity.'[302]

Mohamed Nasreddin reportedly criticized the DoPs, *inter alia*, for not clearly referring to Egypt's historic rights and past agreements, including the 1902 Nile Treaty.[303] Conversely, Minga Negash et al argue that 'the [DoPs] clauses are designed to re-assert the 1929 and 1959 water sharing agreements,' including the 1993 Framework Instrument.[304] However, these two extreme positions do not do justice to the DoPs as the instrument is founded on equitable utilization and participation, guaranteeing the two countries water use rights 'consistent with international law.'[305] This is not to denounce reasoned criticisms of the Declaration. Negash et al, for instance, argue that Article ii of the Declaration 'can be interpreted to exclude ... the use of the waters for fishing, recreation, education and small scale industrial and irrigation projects around the dam' and thus it is 'devoid of shared benefits and responsibilities.'[306] It is doubtful that the DoPs was meant to ban non-harmful use of dam water such as fisheries, tourism and planting trees in the dam area, some activities which were clearly envisaged since the project's inception.[307] However, the DoPs rightly, but controversially, gave an apparent guarantee to Egypt and Sudan that the (key) purpose of the dam is not for irrigation. The DoPs could, however, be said to be unfair for Ethiopia as the full costs of the project are to be met from its state and citizens' coffers,[308] while the benefits will be shared with others. Egypt has managed to block all avenues of external funds for the GERD,[309] despite some early reports suggesting that it offered to help

302 Franck, supra note 28, p. 56.

303 See, 'Al-Sisi Criticised for Waiving Egypt's Right Over Nile Water,' *Middle Eastern Monitor* (23 March 2015), retrieved from https://www.middleeastmonitor.com/news/africa/17657.

304 M. Negash, S. Hassan, M. Muchie & A. Girma, 'Perspectives on the Declaration of Principles Regarding the Grand Ethiopian Renaissance Dam,' *The Thinker*, Vol. 65 (2015), pp. 56–61.

305 See, H. Afifi, 'Egyptian Experts Divided Over Renaissance Dam Declaration of Principles,' *Ahramonline* (24 March 2015), retrieved from http://english.ahram.org.eg/News/126005.aspx.

306 Negash et al, supra note 304.

307 See, *Grand Ethiopian Renaissance Dam*, EEPCo (Ethiopian Electric Power Corporation), retrieved from http://www.eepco.gov.et/abouttheproject.php?pid=1&pcatid=2.

308 MIT Report, supra note 10.

309 See, 'A Dam Nuisance: Egypt and Ethiopia Quarrel Over Water,' *The Economist* (20 April 2011), retrieved from http://www.economist.com/node/18587195.

financially.[310] Egypt's policy on external finance for upstream projects does not appear to have been discontinued post-DoPs. In this context one may question whether the deal made to export electricity to Egypt as a matter of priority is a fair deal for Ethiopia, although this will depend on the price, which is yet to be fixed. As the filling, operation and flow of the dam might be heavily or lightly regulated in the interest of Egypt and Sudan, some level of cost sharing would be imperative as part of a fair deal. With respect to the Owen Falls Dam in Uganda, Egypt was subjected to a 4.5 million Egyptian pounds expenditure to cover the costs of the dam in return, *inter alia*, for direct control of the flow of the dam.[311]

Dam Operation and Filling

To introduce a fair deal relating to the filling and operation of GERD requires an agreement on relevant principles and specific rules and guidelines. Article V of the DoPs, titled 'Principle to cooperate on the First Filling and Operation of the Dam,' should be the basis to consider what a fair filling and operation will look like.

Dam Operation

Paragraph 'b' of Article V stipulates that the three countries 'agree on guidelines and rules for the annual operation of GERD, which the owner of the dam may adjust from time to time.' Under paragraph 'c' of the same article it is further provided that 'to sustain cooperation and coordination on the annual operation of GERD with downstream reservoirs, the three countries, through the line ministries responsible for water, shall set up an appropriate coordination mechanism among them.' In addition to the agreement on setting up suitable institutional mechanisms, this article expressly recognizes (a) the need for coordination between the operation of the GERD and downstream dams and (b) the interests of both upstream and downstream parties, with the owner exercising some discretion to make adjustments on agreed operation plans. The studies to be conducted based upon the recommendations of the IPoE will, and should, feed into rules and modalities of dam operation and coordination to be agreed upon by the three countries.

---

310 A. Maasho, 'INSIGHT-Paying for Giant Nile Dam Itself, Ethiopia Thwarts Egypt but Takes Risks,' *Reuters* (23 April 2014), retrieved from http://www.reuters.com/article/ethiopia-energy-idUSL6N0N91QM20140423#oyFaPZTMs1UPhfBG.97.

311 Woldetsadik, supra note 128, p. 41.

Making dam operation arrangements in line with the spirit of distributive justice will not be an easy matter. Egypt[312] and Sudan might claim that the operation of the dam with respect to water flow regulation must not affect their current or historic use as set out in colonial-era Nile treaties, although this is in conflict with the underlying principles adopted in the DoPs. Instead, Ethiopia will most likely rely on its customary international law entitlement to equitable use, as also accepted by the three parties. The 2014 MIT Report on this question stresses that operations of the GERD and downstream reservoirs ought to be coordinated 'to ensure that economic and financial benefits are realized, and that the waters are equitably shared among all users.'[313]

Ethiopia has to operate and use the dam in compliance with the duty to prevent significant harm on Sudan and Egypt. Customary international law, the DoPs and Ethiopia itself recognize this obligation. The MIT Report further recommends that 'to achieve Ethiopia's "no harm" goal, it is important that the GERD, AHD, and Sudan's reservoirs be operated in coordination by Egypt, Ethiopia, and Sudan.'[314] Ethiopia has reiterated that it neither intends to harm Egypt and Sudan nor have the studies indicated negative impacts. GERD's purpose and suitability is for hydropower generation; once the reservoir is filled, 'Ethiopia will want to maintain large releases of water through the turbines in order to maximize its hydropower revenues.'[315] Apart from safety and similar issues, as considered above, therefore, the potential of significant harm from GERD as a result of reduced water flow is remote in normal (excluding drought-like) dam operation conditions. The MIT Report supports this assertion, concluding that 'most of the time there will be relatively little conflict between Ethiopia's desire to maximize the value of the GERD's hydropower production and the water requirements of downstream users.'[316] Thus, the question of harm arising from dam operation and water flow regulation, as an aspect of distributive justice, appears to be academic.

Dam Filling

In contrast to dam operations, GERD's reservoir filling poses immediate and practical concerns to the dam owner and the two downstream countries respectively. The MIT Report meticulously summarizes this tension as follows:

---

312 Aman, supra note 226.

313 MIT Report, supra note 10, p. 3.

314 Ibid.

315 Ibid., p. 6.

316 Ibid., p. 4.

> Both Sudan and Egypt should be especially interested in GERD releases during filling and periods of drought, because at these times the interests of the downstream riparians differ from those of Ethiopia. Egypt and Sudan need releases from the GERD to meet minimum water requirements, but Ethiopia may prefer to increase the quantity of water stored in the GERD reservoir.[317]

Dam filling and coordination of different reservoirs during filling are largely technical matters. The basis of a fair legal and policy option for the GERD filling are of interest here. Article V of the DoPs provides that

> [t]he Three Countries, in the spirit of cooperation, will utilize the final outcomes of the joint studies, to be conducted as per the recommendations of the IPoE Report and agreed upon by the TNC, to ... agree on guidelines and rules on the first filling of GERD which shall cover all different scenarios, in parallel with the construction of GERD.[318]

Until now no agreement has been reached on dam filling guidelines and rules for the GERD by the three countries.[319] However, the 2014 MIT Report and subsequently published scholarship have dealt with some general and detailed filling scenarios and options for the GERD. The MIT Report, recognizing Ethiopia's natural desire and incentive to fill the dam quickly, and the downstream impacts of such speedy filling, recommended an agreement on dam filling to be flexible and adaptable

> to the actual sequence of Nile flows that occurs while the GERD reservoir is filling. It must be able to meet the agreed objectives given the many possible conditions of the Eastern Nile water resource each year: AHD reservoir storage level, the GERD storage level and Blue Nile flow. For example, if during filling of the GERD reservoir the AHD is full, Egypt could draw down the AHD reservoir to meet its water requirements as Blue Nile flow is stored in the GERD reservoir, effectively shifting storage upstream and reducing evaporation losses from the AHD reservoir ... However, if the AHD reservoir storage is low, then less Blue Nile flow could be stored

317 Ibid., p. 5.

318 DoPs, supra note 12, Art. V(2)(a).

319 Z. Yihdego, A. Rieu-Clarke & A. Cascão, 'How Has the Grand Ethiopian Renaissance Dam Changed the Legal, Political, Economic and Scientific Dynamics in the Nile Basin?,' *Water International*, Vol. 41(4) (2106), pp. 503–511, p. 507.

> in the GERD reservoir and agreed downstream releases could be made for Egypt and Sudan.... Any filling agreement must have provision for meeting the minimum water requirement for Egypt and Sudan.[320]

In contrast, Zhang, Erkyihun and Block propose a fixed annual or monthly release of water combined with a pre-defined number of years for filling.[321] Unlike the MIT Report, their approach provides specific scenarios and options for GERD filling. Without trying to predict the effects of climate change on the streamflow of the Blue Nile, Zhang et al looked at three fixed filling scenarios and options based on 4, 6 and 8 and 10+ years to fill the dam. The 4 and 10+ years filling options are seen as two extreme options that might be favoured by Ethiopia and downstream countries respectively. The 4-year filling option, as the shortest period of filling, would be beneficial to Ethiopia and yield a prompt return on its huge investment and support its economy. This option will also be beneficial to downstream and other neighbouring countries by getting relatively cheaper electricity from Ethiopia as soon as possible. Sudan's hydropower,[322] and potentially agriculture, will also benefit from GERD's full-scale flow. This option was used when filling the Aswan High Dam in Egypt without causing a major crisis for Egyptian agriculture, hydropower and other economic activities.[323] However, the GERD is built on the Blue Nile which provides around 60% of Nile waters. Egyptian agriculture, fisheries and hydropower might (or might not) sustain significant harm, even temporarily, if Ethiopia fills the GERD over four or less years'.[324] For this reason, this option may not provide a fair result and is less likely to attract consensus from the three countries.

The 10+ years' option is equivalent to a filling of 10% monthly streamflow[325] of the Blue Nile. This filling option will certainly benefit Egypt and perhaps Sudan as the GERD filling would not 'be felt much downstream. In turn, Ethiopia would not get timely investment returns, including satisfying its acute electricity demands, or the returns from the sale of hydropower to neighbouring countries. This option is thus not only detrimental to Ethiopia, but also to the region as it defeats the regional integration aims and objectives of

320 MIT Report, supra note 10, p. 4.

321 Zhang et al, supra note 20, pp. 593–610.

322 Wheeler et al, supra 295, p. 630.

323 It is quite obvious that Egypt could not possibly fill the huge Aswan High Dam reservoir without negatively affecting its irrigated agriculture.

324 Zhang et al, supra note 20, p. 608.

325 Ibid.

the GERD as adopted in the DoPs. This option also fundamentally defeats the essence of distributive justice as it effectively blocks the enjoyment of legal rights by Ethiopia and its people.

It was proposed that the 6- and 8-year filling options, with emphasis on the 6-year' period, which is an average 25% monthly streamflow of the Blue Nile, could serve as a compromise solution.[326] This will enable GERD to generate electricity at full capacity for Ethiopia in the medium term, offer better flow and flood control to Sudan, and provide potentially cheaper electricity and better water flow to Egypt, without causing a significant interruption to the supply needs of downstream communities.

Agreeing on a pre-defined number of years for filling may not be the sole option available; filling may be better implemented through other approaches. For example, the GERD filling scenarios suggested by Wheeler et al' avoid the pre-defined years-based strategy and aim to eliminate 'all risks of the HAD [High Aswan Dam] reaching the minimum power elevation,' which is necessary for both hydropower generation from the AHD and satisfying all other downstream demands, by proposing 35 BCM or more water release per annum from GERD during the filling period.[327] Such a 'middle ground,' they argue, will bring 'increased benefits [for Ethiopia and the region] and reduced downstream risks [for Egypt and Sudan].'[328] This appears to contradict the 'minimum requirement' threshold proposed by the MIT Report. In addition to the fixed options, however, Wheeler et al advocate for agreeing on a 'safeguard policy' to release more water when unplanned shortages or drought occur downstream, in addition to the 35 BCM annual release.[329]

Given that the total GERD's reservoir capacity is 74 BCM, and if the 35 BCM annual release is agreed to, GERD would be less likely to be at full capacity, as conceded by Wheeler et al.[330] Finding a middle ground to addressing the concerns of downstream Egypt and Sudan is essential. Ethiopia should aim to minimize any harm on Egypt and Sudan during GERD filling. However, this must be re-balanced by meeting the legitimate interests of Ethiopia, including its huge unilateral investment and the temporary nature of dam filling. What this means is that it may not necessarily be fair to claim a nearly *status quo* position on water flow during dam filling.

326 Ibid., pp. 600–601.
327 Wheeler et al, *supra* note 295, pp. 611–634.
328 Ibid., pp. 630–631. Clarification added.
329 Ibid.
330 Ibid.

The legal basis for filling, similar to that of dam operation, must be based on the principles adopted in the DoPs and in customary international law—equitable use, no significant harm, cooperation—and absolutely not on existing water-quota-based colonial-era treaties. In addition to, at least, making sure that minimum water supply to Egypt and Sudan is maintained during GERD filling, vital human needs (such as water supply for drinking and sanitation and arguably for subsistence farming)[331] must not be affected at any time during dam filling. Affecting such vital needs through human conduct would not serve distributive justice for Sudan and Egypt and their communities. This approach should also be adhered to after the end of dam filling.

The issue of dam filling and dam operation are crucial to understanding the distributive justice results of the GERD. Both issues require informed decision making and (flexible) agreement. While scholars and consultancy firms may provide some options and scenarios, a fair deal can only be obtained through good faith negotiations. As there is no rigid qualitative or empirical formula that can be used to implement fairness for the three countries, some compromises must be made to balance the costs and benefits of the filling and operation of the GERD. Such compromises must take into account situations of drought, water availability in Sudanese and Egyptian reservoirs, and wetter and drier seasons so as to prevent significant harm downstream. This ought to be done on the firm basis, as required by the DoPs, that filling, operation and utilization of GERD in a coordinated fashion will bring a fair result to the three countries, their communities, the region and the natural environment.[332] This is not necessarily going to be an easy task to accomplish.

Hopes and Challenges of Ensuring Distributive Justice

The tripartite recognition of the core principles of customary watercourses law, supported by further details of operation and management of the GERD must be commended as a step in the right direction of ensuring distributive

---

331 UNWC, supra note 65, Article 10 on the 'Relationship between different kinds of uses' states:

> In the absence of agreement or custom to the contrary, no use of an international watercourse enjoys inherent priority over other uses.
>
> In the event of a conflict between uses of an international watercourse, it shall be resolved with reference to articles 5 to 7, with special regard being given to the requirements of *vital human needs*. (Italics added).

332 This approach is adopted for example in the Southern African Development Communities (SADAC) region. See, Revised Protocol on Shared Watercourses in the Southern African Development Community (7 August 2000), Art. 2(c), retrieved from http://www.sadc.int/files/3413/6698/6218/Revised_Protocol_on_Shared_Watercourses_-_2000_-_English.pdf.

justice. Yet translating the details for equitable use and preventing significant harm into specific actions will be a delicate matter be it in relation to dam filling, dam operation or in general terms. Two examples are offered to illustrate this challenge generally. The first is the issue of how to assess the water needs of downstream Egypt (and Sudan) and upstream Ethiopia. With respect to meeting the water needs, following the signing of the DoPs, Egyptian President Al-Sisi told the Ethiopian Parliament in March 2015:

> I invite you today to jointly lay the foundations of a better future for our children and grandchildren, a future where all the classrooms in Ethiopia are lit and all the children of Egypt can drink from the River Nile as their fathers and grandfathers did.[333]

This is consistent with long-standing policy of Egypt which regards the Nile as a matter of life and death for Egypt, but an issue of development or energy provision for Ethiopia.[334] The Nile is undoubtedly vital for the livelihood and the existence of millions of Egyptians, although it is well documented that Egypt also has renewable and non-renewable groundwater (aquifer) resources which can supplement current Nile water uses.[335]

The president's characterization of the water needs of both countries, if only applicable to the GERD, seems reasonable. However, that does not seem to be the case if the statement is read in conjunction with the Egyptian Constitution and policy. If this determination on the water needs of the parties is correct, either in its most limited or broadest sense, it would be in the interest of distributive justice to give priority to Egypt (and Sudan) over Ethiopia and the other upstream countries' water needs. Any use of Nile waters contrary to 'vital human needs' of downstream populations would contravene the distributive

333 'See, 'Egypt Stresses Nile Water Rights in Ethiopia Dam Project,' *Daily Mail* (25 March 2015), retrieved from http://www.dailymail.co.uk/wires/afp/article-3011635/Egypt-stresses-Nile-water-rights-Ethiopia-dam-project.html.

334 Egypt's Perspective, supra 'note 5.

335 H. I. Abdel-Shafy & R. O. Aly, 'Water Issue in Egypt: Resources, Pollution and Protection Endeavours,' *Central European Journal of Occupational and Environmental Medicine*, Vol. 8(1) (2002), pp. 3–21, retrieved from http://www.omfi.hu/cejoem/Volume8/Vol8No1/CE02_1-01.html; G. G. E. Eckstein, *Hydrologic Reality: International Water Law and Transboundary Ground-Water Resources*, paper and lecture for the conference on 'Water: Dispute Prevention and Development' (American University Centre for the Global South, Washington, D.C., 12–13 October 1998).

justice component of fairness.[336] The GERD National Panel of Expert, however, asserts that

> of all African Countries, surely of all Nile Basin countries, it is only Egypt that has over 98% of its population with access to potable water, while an Ethiopian girl of sixteen has to go on average 6 kilometres each day back and forth to fetch a gallon of water from a river or a dug hole.[337]

It must be noted that fetching water is only possible in Ethiopia if it is available on the ground, which entirely relies on adequate rainfall.

The second example concerns the challenge of applying socio-economic needs as a factor for determining equitable water use for Egypt and Ethiopia. In articulating why Ethiopia 'won' the diplomatic and legal battle regarding the GERD, Salman argues:

> Ethiopia has relied in its strategy on the fairness of its cause as it is the source of 86% of the Nile water while it uses only 1% of that Nile water. Yet it continued undergoing successive famines, especially those of 1983–85 which claimed about a million lives, in addition to the crushing poverty the Ethiopian people are suffering from.[338]

Once again Ethiopia is trying to heal its wounds from a severe drought which has affected millions of its citizens.[339] This is likely to reoccur unless the country's total dependency on rainfall for agriculture ceases.

Undeniably, Egypt is richer than Ethiopia in food security, drinking water availability and economic development. Recent data shows that Egypt's per capita income for 2015 was US$3,614.70 while Ethiopia's was US$619.2.[340] Extreme poverty in upstream countries, including Ethiopia, is ubiquitous; lack of classrooms and home lighting in most parts of rural Ethiopia are just

---

336 UNWC, supra note 65, Art. 10.

337 'A Proxy Campaign against Ethiopia? A Response by GERD National Panel of Experts (NPoE)' *EIPSA Communicating Article*, Vol. 1(3) (April 2014), pp. 1–9, p. 5, retrieved from http://www.eipsa1.com/cms/articles/GERDFINALNPOERebuttalIRN.pdf.

338 S. Salman, 'How and Why Has the Ethiopian Strategy on the Renaissance Dam Succeeded?,' *Sudan Vision* (25 May 2015), retrieved from http://news.sudanvisiondaily.com/details.html?rsnpid=248051.

339 C. Myrie, 'El Nino Threatens "'Millions in East and Southern Africa,'" *BBC News* (10 November 2015), retrieved from http://www.bbc.co.uk/news/uk-34779447.

340 *GDP per capita* (2010–2014 Data), World Bank, retrieved from http://data.worldbank.org/indicator/NY.GDP.PCAP.CD.

part of the problem. Millions of Ethiopians need food, basic clothing, shelter and health services, despite the economic progress made in recent years. This means that Ethiopia's need to use the Blue Nile (or other tributaries) is neither a luxury nor limited to generating electricity.

Such apparent inequality between Egypt and Ethiopia may be accepted or accommodated for the reason that distributive justice 'recognizes' or appreciates disparity in countries' wealth and development as an inevitable fact.[341] International (watercourses) law firmly favours 'the achievement of more rational and equitable international economic relations.'[342] It is doubtful that the DoPs impliedly endorses inequality as a factor for sharing Nile resources. Whatever the position of the law may be on inequality, the principle of fairness requires working towards narrowing the gap in wealth distribution.[343]

The post-1990 undertakings are different from the old Nile treaties in that they aim to address the fairness dilemma; given the uncertainties surrounding them, however, it may be a question as to whether they are part of the problem. As the final part of this monograph demonstrates, however, they can offer a path out from the fairness dilemma in the sharing of water resources in the Nile Basin.

Concluding Remarks: Lessons to be Learnt?

After a careful analysis of the salient features of justice, equity and fairness, it is clear that fairness provides a solid legal basis to the sharing of transboundary resources. More specifically, the UNWC and basin-specific (existing or emerging) regimes such as the CFA, represent a fair system for sharing transboundary water resources. Such a system contests the (unjustified) rejection of distributive justice and its narrow construction in the equity discourse. As the eastern Nile Basin countries are not parties to the UNWC and the CFA (except Ethiopia), Franck's theory of fairness has been tested with particular reference

341 See 'Features and Challenges' in this monograph.

342 Charter of Economic Rights, supra note 56, preamble. The Charter asserts, under Article 2(1), on the one hand, that '[e]very State has and shall freely exercise full permanent sovereignty, including possession, use and disposal, over all its wealth, natural resources and economic activities.' Under Article 3, on the other hand, it states: 'In the exploitation of natural resources shared by two or more countries, each State must co-operate on the basis of a system of information and prior consultations in order to achieve optimum use of such resources without causing damage to the legitimate interest of others.'

343 Franck, supra note 28.

to the fairness of the GERD from colonial-era Nile treaties, post-1990 commitments and customary international law perspectives. Five concluding remarks can be drawn from the in-depth analysis made of the various instruments and applicable customary rules.

First, despite the use of Nile colonial-era treaties to challenge the procedural and substantive fairness of the GERD, they are not compatible with the dictates of fairness. The real question or dilemma is whether they still exist or ended with the adoption of the DoPs. One observation may be that they are still alive and violated by the GERD project.[344] The opposite and perhaps stronger observation is that, as they are totally rejected by most Nile co-riparians, as both procedurally and substantively flawed instruments, they cannot provide a fair system for sharing Nile resources. Clearly they are not suitable as a basis for compromise and negotiations. It follows from this that the fairness of the GERD[345] cannot be questioned on the basis of these treaties. In fact, the real question now is whether the signing of the DoPs and the endorsement of the GERD by all Nile riparians, notably Sudan and Egypt, has terminated the colonial-era Nile treaties. This includes the 1959 Nile Treaty, which is at odds with the DoPs, the 1993 Framework Instrument, newly-emerging Nile Basin initiatives, and conventional and customary international watercourses law. The lesson here should be that unfair laws and practices cannot be considered as valid merely on technical (or procedural) grounds in modern international law.

Second, there is the question of whether the 1993 and 2015 commitments, in contrast to the old Nile treaties, support or challenge the fairness of building, filling, operating and sharing the costs and benefits of the GERD. The 1993 Framework Instrument aims to promote joint studies for utilizing Nile waters without providing specific and complete procedural and substantive rules This makes it either less attractive to assess the fairness of GERD or a commitment entirely disregarded by both parties as a result of the dominant practice of unilateralism rather than genuine cooperation in the (eastern) Nile Basin. Thus, it became, although not at the level of the older treaties, part of the fairness dilemma, rather than resolving that dilemma. However, the 2015 instrument (DoPs), either as a legally-binding commitment or declaratory of conventional and customary rules, has changed the rules of the game in the use of Nile waters for the better. The impact of this development on the fairness question is twofold. First, unlike colonial-era treaties, and to some extent, the 1993

344 See, Group of Nile Basin (GNB) at Cairo University to Support Egypt, *Cairo University's Report on Ethiopia's Great Renaissance Dam*, Egyptian Chronicles (29 September 2013), retrieved from http://web.mit.edu/12.000/www/m2017/pdfs/ethiopia/cairo.pdf.

345 MIT Report, supra note 10, p. 11.

Instrument, the DoPs has secured the full participation of the three main Nile riparians; their endeavour was assisted by an IPoE and by international firms in the quest to find a win-win, proportionate and fair deal on the basis of modern principles of international watercourses law. Furthermore, the mechanisms introduced to implement the Declaration, ranging from establishing joint national technical committees to meetings of heads of state/government, together with the specific commitment to exchange information, are significant achievements of cooperation. Clearly, these actions fulfil the dictates of procedural fairness as all the parties, supported by international actors, are participating on an equal footing. Second, the substance of the Declaration, comprising the principles of equitable use, no significant harm, sustainable use, protecting the environment, dam safety and clean energy sharing, reflect the hopes and fears of all the parties and signify a system of distributive justice. For these reasons the DoPs, as an initial but a significant step in the right direction, meets the test of 'perceived fairness.'[346] In effect, this makes the GERD as a classic example of fairness in action and the DoPs as the best, if not absolute, tool adopted to unlock the fairness dilemma in the (eastern) Nile Basin.

Third, this unprecedented development has, however, encountered multifaceted challenges, which range from a lack of shared understanding on relevant factors for equitable use, notable water and socio-economic needs of the parties involved, contested claims over the effects and benefits, to resistance to change from both ends (excluding Sudan). In particular, dam filling, dam operation and associated studies are leading to major differences between Egypt, Sudan and Ethiopia. It must be emphasized that maximizing the benefits of the GERD while preventing and reducing potential consequences, as key components of the GERD's fairness, can only be achieved if the three countries maintain the momentum of cooperation and promote reasonable benefit sharing,[347] which should underpin existing projects of cooperation such as the NBI. This provides both the opportunity and the challenge to permanently eliminate extreme claims and counterclaims for Nile water resources. This requires clearing the current tense political atmosphere and keeping up the momentum of good faith negotiations and cooperation.

Fourth, the two instruments signed in the last two to three decades represent the aspirations of the parties to cooperate at the Basin level. In particular, the DoPs' ambition to promote 'transboundary cooperation and regional

346 Franck, supra note 28, p. 13.

347 C. W. Sadoff & D. Grey, 'Beyond the River: The Benefits of Cooperation on International Rivers,' *Water Policy*, Vol. 4 (2002), pp. 389–403.

integration,'[348] along with its endorsement of all the principles of the 2010 CFA, is a positive step towards regional cooperation. Yet there has been no signal sent to expand this fair system to Basin-level collaboration.[349] Tanzania's immediate ratification of the CFA after the 'DoPs was signed ought to be noted; other Basin countries may follow suit. This raises the question, if Egypt and Sudan signed the DoPs, why not the CFA 2010?

One theory may be that they do not want to put legal constraints on their current use of Nile waters, assuming that the DoPs is not a hard law. The other more persuasive theory is that what has already been agreed to with respect to the GERD represents contemporary legal principles and practices that are beneficial to all Nile co-riparians for securing their water share and for being notified and consulted on future planned measures, through appropriate basin-wide or regional institutional framework, which will end existing unilateral practices and contentious projects. Such a Basin-level approach would also lead to fairer results on the river and the environment, with good returns to all. This is notwithstanding the need for global cooperation and the likelihood that (some) Nile Basin states may seriously consider acceding to the UNWC. The message here is, therefore, that while the bottom-up approach to fostering fairness is necessary, such endeavours need to be reinforced by global, regional or basin-wide legal frameworks for cooperation, coordination and sustainable use of resources.

Finally, this monograph has demonstrated that without looking into the way in which laws come into being and the nature of their specific content on a case-by-case basis, it is difficult, if not impossible, to judge them as just or unjust under contemporary international law. For example, Article 3(1) of the UNWC appears to respect the integrity and validity of existing treaties among states when becoming parties to the Convention, although paragraph 2 of the same article offers the option for harmonization. What if an existing agreement between two or more states is at odds with the fundamentals of the Convention itself and general international law? Would they be able to join the UNWC? Some would like to interpret this[350] as an absolute safeguard clause to prior or future water agreements, unless concerned parties wilfully opt for harmonizing such agreements with the terms and spirit of the UNWC. The International Law Commission rightly clarified this question, within the spirit of paragraph 4 of the same article:

348 DoPs, supra note 12, Art. II.

349 Kimenyi & Mbaku, supra note 121.

350 See, e.g., Aal, supra note 156, pp. 28–29.

> [I]f a watercourse agreement is concerned with only part of the watercourse or only a particular project, programme or use relating thereto, it must be subject to the proviso that the use, by one or more other watercourse States not parties to the agreement, of the waters of the watercourse is not, to a significant extent, adversely affected by the agreement. Otherwise, a few States of a multi-State international watercourse could appropriate a disproportionate amount of its benefits for themselves or unduly prejudice the use of its waters by watercourse States not parties to the agreement in question. Such results would run counter to fundamental principles which will be shown to govern the non-navigational uses of international watercourses, such as the right of all watercourse States to use an international watercourse in an equitable and reasonable manner and the obligation not to use a watercourse in such a way as to injure other watercourse States.[351]

This has a wider connotation in international law. If a treaty or custom is failing to meet the test of fairness in both its aspects, taking into account, historical, societal and legal developments in a given field, it has to be disbanded or revised.

As fairness can be relative, it is imperative to distinguish between making laws fairer and better in general terms from dealing with existing laws that defeat, *inter alia*, equality, sovereignty and equity, the key constituents of fairness. This may be criticized as a source of uncertainty in international law by those who overly rely on formalism and treaty (un)making and retaining techniques. However, those who see international law as a dynamic subject will argue that a formal process may not necessarily be procedurally fair; even if it is so, the content may or may not be fair. If law is not flexible enough to adapt to changes and to correct historic or existing unfairness in all its forms, it will cause more *havoc* than stability in the international community in general and in affected regions in particular. This key lesson from the developments in the Nile is something international law cannot afford to ignore. Doing so may further destabilize the international legal system and erode confidence of community of states and their populations on the system, as justly envisaged and theorised by the great public international law scholar, Thomas Franck.[352]

---

351 International Law Commission, *Draft Articles on the Law of the Non-navigational Uses of International Watercourses and Commentaries Thereto and Resolution on Transboundary Confined Groundwater, 1994* (United Nations, 2005), pp. 93–94, retrieved from http://legal.un.org/ilc/texts/instruments/english/commentaries/8_3_1994.pdf.

352 Franck, *supra* note 28, p. 7.

List of References

552 Parl. Deb., H.C. (5th ser.) (18 May 1956) cc2375–412 (Nile Waters), sec 2395, retrieved from http://hansard.millbanksystems.com/commons/1956/may/18/nile-waters#column_2395.

'A Dam Nuisance: Egypt and Ethiopia Quarrel Over Water,' *The Economist* (20 April 2011), retrieved from http://www.economist.com/node/18587195.

'A Proxy Campaign against Ethiopia? A Response by GERD National Panel of Experts (NPoE)' *EIPSA Communicating Article*, Vol. 1(3) (April 2014), pp. 1–9, retrieved from http://www.eipsa1.com/cms/articles/GERDFINALNPOERebuttalIRN.pdf.

Aal, M. S. 'Equitable and Reasonable Utilization of International Rivers in the UN Convention with a Particular Reference to the River Nile,' *African Perspectives*, Vol. 11(39) (2013), pp. 22–28.

Abdelatti, A. 'Egypt's Sisi Denies Supporting Opposition in Ethiopia,' *Reuters* (13 October 2016), retrieved from http://uk.reuters.com/article/uk-ethiopia-unrest-egypt-idUKKCN12D2L5.

Abdel-Shafy, H. I., & R. O. Aly, 'Water Issue in Egypt: Resources, Pollution and Protection Endeavours,' *Central European Journal of Occupational and Environmental Medicine*, Vol. 8(1) (2002), pp. 3–21, retrieved from http://www.omfi.hu/cejoem/Volume8/Vol8No1/CE02_1-01.html.

Abdo, M. 'The Nile Question: The Accords on the Water of the Nile and Their Implications on Cooperative Schemes in the Basin,' *Perceptions–Journal of International Affairs*, Vol. 9(2) (Summer 2004), pp. 45–57, retrieved from http://sam.gov.tr/wp-content/uploads/2012/01/4.-Mohammed-Abdo.pdf.

Abulwafa, A. 'Commitment of International Conventions on the River Nile,' *African Perspectives*, Vol. 11(39) (2013), pp. 7–13.

Act to amend the National Dam Safety Program Act to reauthorize the national dam safety program, and for other purposes, 22 December 2006, Public Law 109–460 [USA], retrieved from https://www.congress.gov/109/plaws/publ460/PLAW-109publ460.pdf.

Aegean Sea Continental Shelf Case (Greece v Turkey), [1978] ICJ Reports 3.

Afifi, H. 'Egyptian Experts Divided Over Renaissance Dam Declaration of Principles,' *Ahramonline* (24 March 2015), retrieved from http://english.ahram.org.eg/News/126005.aspx.

Agreement on Declaration of Principles between the Arab Republic of Egypt, the Federal Democratic Republic of Ethiopia and the Republic of the Sudan on the Grand Ethiopian Renaissance Dam Project (GERDP), 23 March 2015, retrieved from http://hornaffairs.com/en/2015/03/25/egypt-ethiopia-sudan-agreement-on-declaration-of-principles-full-text/.

Agreement on the Nile River Basin Cooperative Framework, May 2010, retrieved from http://www.nilebasin.org/images/docs/CFA%20-%20English%20%20French Version.pdf.

Akehurst, M. 'Equity and General Principles of Law,' *International and Comparative Law Quarterly*, Vol. 25(4) (1976), pp. 801–825.

'Al-Sisi Criticised for Waiving Egypt's Right Over Nile Water,' *Middle Eastern Monitor* (23 March 2015), retrieved from https://www.middleeastmonitor.com/news/africa/17657.

Ali, N. 'Ethiopia Accuses Egypt of Destabilizing the Country by Supporting Rebels,' *Middle East Observer* (11 October 2016).

Allan, J. A., & N. Mirumachi, 'Why Negotiate? Asymmetric Endowments, Asymmetric Power and the Invisible Nexus of Water, Trade and Power That Bring Apparent Water Security,' *in*, A. Earle, A. Jägerskog & J. Őjendal, *Transboundary Water Management: Principles and Practice*, pp. 13–26 (London: Earthscan, 2010).

Altsom, 'Alstom to Supply Hydroelectric Equipment for the Grand Renaissance Dam in Ethiopia,' Press Release (7 January 2013), retrieved from http://www.alstom.com/press-centre/2013/1/alstom-to-supply-hydroelectric-equipment-for-the-grand-renaissance-dam-in-ethiopia/.

Aman, A. 'Egypt Warily Signs Preliminary Nile Agreement,' *Al-monitor* (31 March 2015), retrieved from http://www.al-monitor.com/pulse/originals/2015/03/egypt-eastern-nile-water-agreement-ethiopia-sudan.html#.

Aman, A. 'In Switch, Egypt May Join Ethiopia in Nile Dam Project,' *Al-monitor* (21 October 2013), retrieved from http://www.al-monitor.com/pulse/originals/2013/10/egypt-ethiopia-dam-reconciliation.html#ixzz4UK9hCjUq.

Berhane, D. 'Ethiopia Dismisses International Rivers as Egypt's Proxy,' *Horn Affairs English* (11 April 2014), retrieved from http://hornaffairs.com/en/2014/04/11/ethiopia-dismisses-international-rivers-as-egypts-proxy-full-text-included/.

Birnie, P., A. Boyle & C. Redgwell, *International Law and the Environment, 3rd ed.* (Cambridge: Cambridge University Press, 2009).

Boh, E. 'Ethiopia Accuses Egypt of "Fueling" Violence,' *Africanews* (10 October 2016), retrieved from http://www.africanews.com/2016/10/10/ethiopia-accuses-egypt-of-fueling-violence/.

Boyle, A., & C. Chinkin, *The Making of International Law* (Oxford: Oxford University Press, 2009).

Brownlie, I. *Legal Status of Natural Resources in International Law (Some Aspects)* (*Volume 162*) (Leiden: Brill Nijhoff, 1979).

Brunnée, J., & S. J. Toope, 'The Changing Nile Basin Regime: Does Law Matter?,' *Harvard International Law Journal*, Vol. 43(1) (2002), pp. 105–159.

Cairo Declaration on Border Disputes among African States Legitimising National Borders Inherited from Colonial Times, Organization for African Unity, 1964.

Cascão, A. E. 'Changing Power Relations in the Nile River Basin: Unilateralism vs. Cooperation?,' Water Alternatives, Vol. 2(2) (2009), pp. 245–268.

Cascão, A. E., & A. Nicol, 'GERD: New Norms of Cooperation in the Nile Basin?,' *Water International*, Vol. 41(4) (2016), pp. 559–560.

Case Concerning Maritime Delimitation and Territorial Questions Between Qatar And Bahrain (*Qatar v Bahrain*), Judgement of 1 July 1994 (Jurisdiction and Admissibility), [1994] ICJ Reports 112.

Case Concerning Military and Paramilitary Activities in and Against Nicaragua (*Nicaragua v United States of America*), Judgement of 27 June 1986 (Merits), [1986] ICJ Reports 14.

Case Concerning Pulp Mills on the River Uruguay (*Argentina v Uruguay*), Judgment of 20 April 2010, Separate Opinion of Judge Trindade, [2010] ICJ Reports.

Case Concerning the Barcelona Traction, Light and Power Company, Limited (*Belgium v Spain*), Second Phase Judgment of 5 February 1970, [1970] ICJ Reports 3.

Case Concerning the Continental Shelf (*Tunisia/Libyan Arab Jamahiriya*), Vol. 1, Judgment of 24 February 1982, [1985] ICJ Reports 13.

Case Concerning the Frontier Dispute (*Burkina Faso/Republic of Mali*), Judgment of 22 December 1986, [1986] ICJ Reports 554.

Case Concerning the Gabčikovo-Nagymaros Project (*Hungary v Slovakia*), Judgement of 25 September 1997, [1997] ICJ Reports 7.

Case Concerning the Gabčikovo-Nagymaros Project (*Hungary v Slovakia*), Judgement of 25 September 1997, Separate Opinion of Judge Bedjaoui, [1997] ICJ Reports.

Case Concerning the Land and Maritime Boundary Between Cameroon and Nigeria (*Cameroon v Nigeria: Equatorial Guinea intervening*), [2002] ICJ Reports 303.

Case Relating to the Territorial Jurisdiction of International Commission of the River Oder (*United Kingdom v Poland*), PCIJ Series A No 23, Annex 3 (Order made on 20 August 1929).

Centre of Judicial Studies and Research of the State Council, 'Final Recommendations of the Conference on Nile Basin Agreements in Light of the Provisions of the International Law,' *African Perspectives*, Vol. 11(39) (2013), pp. 68–70.

Charter of Economic Rights and Duties of States, 12 December 1974, Resolution 3281 (XXIX), United Nations General Assembly.

Charter of the United Nations, 24 October 1945

Constitution of the Arab Republic of Egypt, 18 January 2014, retrieved from http://www.sis.gov.eg/Newvr/Dustor-en001.pdf.

Constitutive Act of the African Union, 11 July 2000, retrieved from https://au.int/web/sites/default/files/pages/32020-file-constitutiveact_en.pdf

Convention on the Cooperation for the Protection and Sustainable Use of the Danube River, 29 June 1994, entered into force 22 October 1998, OJ L342 (12 December 1997), retrieved from https://www.icpdr.org/main/icpdr/danube-river-protection-convention.

Convention on the Law of the Non-navigational Uses of International Watercourses, 21 May 1997, entered into force 17 August 2014, United Nations General Assembly, Resolution 51/229 (8 July 1997), 36 *ILM* 700 (1997).

Craven, M. C. R. 'The Problem of State Succession and the Identity of States under International Law,' *European Journal of International Law*, Vol. 9 (1998), pp. 142–162.

Crawford, J. *Brownlie's Principles of Public International Law, 8th ed.* (Oxford: Oxford University Press, 2012).

Declaration on Principles of International Law concerning Friendly Relations and Co-operation among States in accordance with the Charter of the United Nations, 24 October 1970, Resolution 2625 (XXV), United Nations General Assembly.

Declaration on the Granting of Independence to Colonial Countries and Peoples, 14 December 1960, Resolution 1514 (XV), United Nations General Assembly.

Degefu, G. T. *The Nile: Historical, Legal and Developmental Perspectives* (New York: Trafford Publishing, 2003).

Dellapenna, J. W. 'The Customary International Law of Transboundary Fresh Waters,' *International Journal of Global Environmental Issues*, Vol. 1 (3–4) (2001), pp. 264–305.

Dispute Regarding Navigational and Related Rights (*Costa Rica v Nicaragua*), Judgement of 13 July 2009, [2009] ICJ Reports 213.

Eckstein, G. G. E. *Hydrologic Reality: International Water Law and Transboundary Ground-Water Resources*, paper and lecture for the conference on 'Water: Dispute Prevention and Development' (American University Centre for the Global South, Washington, D.C., 12–13 October 1998).

'Egypt Announces Postponement of GERD Impact Studies Contracts Signing,' *Ahramonline* (4 September 2016), retrieved from http://english.ahram.org.eg/News/242347.aspx.

'Egypt, Ethiopia, Sudan Sign Final Contracts on Nile Dam Studies,' *Ahramonline* (20 September 2016), retrieved from http://english.ahram.org.eg/News/244290.aspx.

'Egypt Forced to Negotiate on Nile Dam,' *Stratfor* (20 March 2015), retrieved from https://www.stratfor.com/sample/analysis/egypt-forced-negotiate-nile-dam.

Egypt State Information Service, 'Egypt's Perspective towards the Ethiopian Grand Renaissance Dam Project (GERDP),' *allAfrica* (7 December 2015), retrieved from http://allafrica.com/stories/201512072751.html.

'Egypt Stresses Nile Water Rights in Ethiopia Dam Project,' *Daily Mail* (25 March 2015), retrieved from http://www.dailymail.co.uk/wires/afp/article-3011635/Egypt-stresses-Nile-water-rights-Ethiopia-dam-project.html.

'Egypt's Sisi denies supporting opposition in Ethiopia,' *Reuters* (13 October 2016).

Eleiba, A. 'Sudanese President Backs Ethiopian Dam Ahead of Nile Talks,' *Ahramonline* (5 December 2013), retrieved from http://english.ahram.org.eg/News/88321.aspx.

'Ethiopia Inaugurates Africa's First Ever Biggest Power Dam,' *Sudan Tribune* (14 November 2009).

'Ethiopia Won't Stop Construction of the Renaissance Dam: Minister,' *Sudan Tribune* (13 February 2016), retrieved from http://www.sudantribune.com/spip.php?article57997.

Ethiopian International Professional Support for Abay, Ethiopian International Professional Support for Abay/Nile (EIPSA), retrieved from http://www.eipsa1.com/cms/.

Ethiopian National Planning Commission, *The Growth and Transformation Plan II* (GTP II), (May 2016).

European Union, Water Framework Directive, 2000/60/EC, 23 October 2000.

Farid, S. 'Will Egypt Still Get Its Fair Share of Nile Water?.' *Al Arabiya News* (31 March 2015), retrieved from http://english.alarabiya.net/en/perspective/analysis/2015/03/31/Will-Egypt-still-get-its-fair-share-of-Nile-water-.html.

Framework for General Co-operation between the Arab Republic of Egypt and Ethiopia, 1 July 1993, UNTS, Vol. 2693, No. 47816, retrieved from http://gis.nacse.org/tfdd/tfdddocs/521ENG.pdf.

Franck, T. *Fairness in International Law and Institutions* (Oxford: Clarendon Press, 1995).

Frontier Dispute (Burkina Faso/Niger), Judgement of 16 April 2013, Separate Opinion of Judge Yusuf, [2013] ICJ Reports.

Garretson, A. H. 'The Nile Basin,' *in*, A. H. Garretson, R. D. Hayton & C. J. Olmstead (eds.), *The Law of International Drainage Basins*, pp. 256–297 (New York: Oceana, 1967).

Garretson, A. H. 'The Nile River System,' *Proceedings of the American Society of International Law*, Vol. 54 (1960), pp. 136–163.

GDP per capita (2010–2014 Data), World Bank, retrieved from http://data.worldbank.org/indicator/NY.GDP.PCAP.CD.

'GERD to Start Generate 750 MW Soon,' *EBC* (15 October 2015), retrieved from http://www.ebc.et/web/ennews/-/gerd-to-start-generate-750-mw-soon.

Goshu, S. 'BRLi, Artelia Get Clearance to Conduct GERD Impact Studies,' *Ethiopian Reporter* (24 September 2016).

Grand Ethiopian Renaissance Dam, EEPCo (Ethiopian Electric Power Corporation), retrieved from http://www.eepco.gov.et/abouttheproject.php?pid=1&pcatid=2.

Gray, C. 'The Use of Force and the International Legal Order,' *in*, M. D. Evans (ed.), *International Law, 3rd ed.*, pp. 615–647 (Oxford: Oxford University Press, 2010).

Grotius, H. *The Law of War and Peace, Book III, Chapter 2, Vol. 1* (1625).

Group of Nile Basin (GNB) at Cairo University to Support Egypt, *Cairo University's Report on Ethiopia's Great Renaissance Dam*, Egyptian Chronicles (29 September 2013), retrieved from http://web.mit.edu/12.000/www/m2017/pdfs/ethiopia/cairo.pdf.

Hammam, H. *A Legal Analysis of the Declaration of Principles on the Grand Ethiopian Renaissance Dam*, Public International Law Blog, retrieved from https://law4371.wordpress.com/2015/05/08/a-legal-analysis-of-the-declaration-of-principles-on-the-grand-ethiopian-renaissance-dam/.

Hashim, A. 'The Egyptian Military, Part Two: From Mubarak Onward,' *Middle East Policy*, Vol. 18(4) (Winter 2011).

Hollis, D. B. *The Oxford Guide to Treaties Edited by Bibliographic Information* (Oxford: Oxford University Press, 2012).

Hossain, K. 'The Environmental Law-Making Process,' *in*, S. Alam et al, *Routledge Handbook of International Environmental Law*, pp. 61–76 (Abingdon: Routledge, 2013).

Interim National Constitution of the Republic of Sudan, 6 July 2005.

International Law Commission, *Draft Articles on the Law of the Non-navigational Uses of International Watercourses and Commentaries Thereto and Resolution on Transboundary Confined Groundwater, 1994* (United Nations, 2005), retrieved from http://legal.un.org/ilc/texts/instruments/english/commentaries/8_3_1994.pdf.

International Panel of Experts (IPoE) on Grand Ethiopian Renaissance Dam Project (GERDP) Final Report, (31 May 2013), retrieved from https://www.international-rivers.org/sites/default/files/attached-files/international_panel_of_experts_for_ethiopian_renaissance_dam-_final_report_1.pdf.

Jennings, R. 'Equity and Equidistance Principles,' *Annuaire Suisse de Droit International*, Vol. 27 (1986), pp. 31–35.

Kasimbazi, E. B. 'The Impact of Colonial Agreements on the Regulation of the Waters of the River Nile,' *Water International*, Vol. 35(6) (2010), pp. 718–732. DOI:10.1080/02508060.2010.533642.

Kelley, M. B., & R. Johnson, 'STRATFOR: Egypt is Prepared to Bomb All of Ethiopia's Nile Dams,' *Business Insider* (13 October 2012), retrieved from http://www.businessinsider.com/hacked-stratfor-emails-egypt-could-take-military-action-to-protect-its-stake-in-the-nile-2012-10#ixzz3afm498Zg.

Kimenyi, M., & J. Mbaku, *Governing the Nile River Basin: The Search for a New Legal Regime* (Arlington: Brookings Institution Press, 2015).

Klabbers, J. 'Beyond the Vienna Convention: Conflicting Treaty Provisions,' *in*, E. Cannizzaro (ed.), *The Law of Treaties Beyond the Vienna Convention*, pp. 192–205 (Oxford: Oxford University Press, 2011).

Kritsiotis, D. 'Imagining the International Community,' *European Journal of International Law*, Vol. 13(4) (2002), pp. 961–992.

Lauterpacht, H. *The Function of Law in the International Community* (Oxford: Oxford University Press, 2011).

Leb, C., & M. Tignino, 'State Succession to Water Treaties: Uncertainties and Extremes,' *in*, L. B. Boisson de Chazournes, C. Leb & M. Tignino (eds.), *International Law and Freshwater: The Multiple Challenges*, pp. 421–444 (Cheltenham: Edward Elgar, 2013).

Legal Consequences of the Construction of a Wall in the Occupied Palestinian Territory, Advisory

Legal Status of Eastern Greenland, PCIJ Series A/B No 53 (5 April 1933).

Lie, J. H. S. *Supporting the Nile Basin Initiative: A Political Analysis 'Beyond the River'*, Norwegian Institute of International Affairs (2010), retrieved from http://www.academia.edu/2243972/Supporting_the_Nile_Basin_Initiative_A_Political_Analysis_Beyond_the_River.

Lowe, V. 'The Role of Equity in International Law,' *Australian Yearbook of International Law*, Vol. 12 (1988–89), pp. 54–81.

Lumumba, P. L. O. 'The Interpretation of the 1929 Treaty and its Legal Relevance and Implications for the Stability of the Region,' *African Sociological Review*, 11(1) (2007), pp. 10–24.

Maasho, A. 'INSIGHT-Paying for Giant Nile Dam Itself, Ethiopia Thwarts Egypt but Takes Risks,' *Reuters* (23 April 2014), retrieved from http://www.reuters.com/article/ethiopia-energy-idUSL6N0N91QM20140423#oyFaPZTMs1UPhfBG.97.

Magsig, B.-O. *International Water Law and the Quest for Common Security* (Cheltenham: Routledge, 2015).

Maiese, M. 'Principles of Justice and Fairness,' *in*, G. Burgess & H. Burgess (eds.), *Beyond Intractability* (Boulder: Conflict Information Consortium, University of Colorado, 2003), retrieved from http://www.beyondintractability.org/print/2373.

Malanczuk, P. *Akehurst's Modern Introduction to International Law, 7th ed.* (Cheltenham: Routledge, 1997).

Maluwa, T. *International Law in Post-Colonial Africa* (Leiden: Martinus Nijhoff, 1999).

Martens, E. 'Article 102,' *in*, B. Simma et al, *The Charter of the United Nations: A Commentary, 3rd ed., Volume 2*, pp. 2098–2109 (Oxford: Oxford University Press, 2012).

Matz-Lück, N. 'Framework Conventions as a Regulatory Tool,' *Goettingen Journal of International Law*, Vol. 1(3) (2009), pp. 439–458.

McCaffrey, S. *The Law of International Watercourses, 2nd ed.* (Oxford: Oxford University Press, 1997).

McIntyre, O. 'Utilization of Shared International Freshwater Resources: The Meaning and Role of "Equity" in International Water Law,' *Water International*, Vol. 38(2) (2013), pp. 112–129.

McIntyre, O. *Environmental Protection of International Watercourses under International Law* (Aldershot: Ashgate, 2007).

McKenzie, S. O. 'Egypt's Choice: From the Nile Basin Treaty to the Cooperative Framework Agreement, an International Legal Analysis,' *Transnational Law & Contemporary Problems*, Vol. 21 (2012), pp. 571–599, retrieved from http://papers.ssrn.com/sol3/papers.cfm?abstract_id=2445962.

Mekonnen, D. Z. 'The Nile Basin Cooperative Framework Agreement Negotiations and the Adoption of a "Water Security" Paradigm: Flight into Obscurity or a Logical Cul-de-sac?,' *European Journal of International Law*, Vol. 21(2) (2010), pp. 421–440. DOI: 10.1093/ejil/chq027.

MIT Abdul Latif Jameel World Water and Food Security Lab, *The Grand Ethiopian Renaissance Dam: An Opportunity for Collaboration and Shared Benefits in the*

Eastern Nile Basin, (2014), retrieved from http://jwafs.mit.edu/sites/default/files/documents/GERD_2014_Full_Report.pdf.

Moyle, J. B. *The Institutes of Justinian, 5th ed.* (Oxford: Clarendon Press, 1913), bk I, title 1, retrieved from http://droitromain.upmf-grenoble.fr/Anglica/just1_Moyle.htm.

Myrie, C. 'El Nino Threatens "Millions in East and Southern Africa,'" *BBC News* (10 November 2015), retrieved from http://www.bbc.co.uk/news/uk-34779447.

National Water Act, 6 August 1998, Act No. 36 [South Africa], retrieved from http://www.acts.co.za/national-water-act-1998/.

Negarit Gazeta, 1991–07–22, Vol. 50, No. 1 [Ethiopia], pp. 1–5.

Negash, M., S. Hassan, M. Muchie & A. Girma, 'Perspectives on the Declaration of Principles Regarding the Grand Ethiopian Renaissance Dam,' *The Thinker*, Vol. 65 (2015), pp. 56–61.

Office of National Council for the Coordination of Public Participation on The Grand Renaissance Dam, retrieved from http://www.hidasse.gov.et/.

Okoth-Owiro, A. 'State Succession and International Treaty Commitments: A Case Study of the Nile Water Treaties,' Occasional Paper, East Africa # 9, Konrad Adenauer Stiftung and Law & Policy Foundation (2004), retrieved from http://www.kas.de/wf/doc/kas_6306-544-1-30.pdf.

Paisley, R. K., & T. W. Henshaw, 'Transboundary Governance of the Nile River Basin: Past, Present and Future,' *Environmental Development*, Vol. 7 (July 2013), pp. 59–71.

Permanent Sovereignty Over Natural Resources, 14 December 1962, Resolution 1803 (XVII), United Nations General Assembly.

Prost, M., & A. T. Camprudi, 'Against Fairness? International Environmental Law, Disciplinary Bias and Pareto Justice,' *Leiden Journal of International Law*, Vol. 25(2) (2012), pp. 379–396.

Protocol for Sustainable Development of Lake Victoria Basin, 29 November 2003, retrieved from http://faolex.fao.org/docs/pdf/mul41042.pdf.

Ratner, R. S. *The Thin Justice of International Law: A Moral Reckoning of the Law of Nations* (Oxford: Oxford University Press, 2015).

Ratner, S. 'Drawing a Better Line: UTI Possidetis and the Borders of New States,' *American Journal of International Law*, Vol. 90(4) (1996), pp. 590–624.

Rawls, J. A. 'Justice as Fairness,' *The Philosophical Review*, Vol. 67(2) (1958), pp. 164–194.

Rawls, J. A. *Theory of Justice*, rev. ed. (Cambridge, MA: Harvard University Press, 1999).

Revised Protocol on Shared Watercourses in the Southern African Development Community (7 August 2000), retrieved from http://www.sadc.int/files/3413/6698/6218/Revised_Protocol_on_Shared_Watercourses_-_2000_-_English.pdf.

Rieu-Clarke, A. 'Notification and Consultation on Planned Measures Concerning International Watercourses: Learning from the Pulp Mills and Kishenganga Cases,' *Yearbook of International Environmental Law*, Vol. 24(1) (2014), pp. 102–130.

Rieu-Clarke, A., & G. Pegram, 'Impacts on the International Architecture for Transboundary Waters,' *in*, F. R. Loures & A. Rieu-Clarke, *The UN Watercourses Convention in Force: Strengthening International Law for Transboundary Water Management*, pp. 67–76 (Abingdon: Routledge, 2103).

Sadoff, C. W., & D. Grey, 'Beyond the River: The Benefits of Cooperation on International Rivers,' *Water Policy*, Vol. 4 (2002), pp. 389–403.

Salama, A. 'The Principle of Fundamental Change in Circumstances and its Impact on the Nile Basin Agreements,' *African Perspectives*, Vol. 11(39) (2013), pp. 36–40.

Salman, S. 'Dams, International Rivers, and Riparian States: An Analysis of the Recommendations of the World Commission on Dams,' *American University International Law Review*, Vol. 16(6) (2001), pp. 1477–1505.

Salman, S. 'The Helsinki Rules, the UN Watercourses Convention and the Berlin Rules: Perspectives on International Water Law,' *International Journal of Water Resources Development*, Vol. 23(4) (2007), pp. 625–640.

Salman, S. *The World Bank Policy for Projects on International Waterways: An Historical and Legal Analysis* (Washington, DC: The World Bank, 2009).

Salman, S. 'Downstream Riparians Can Also Harm Upstream Riparians: The Concept of Foreclosure of Future Uses,' *Water International*, Vol. 35(4) (2010), pp. 350–364.

Salman, S. 'The Nile Basin Cooperative Framework Agreement: A Peacefully Unfolding African Spring?,' *Water International*, Vol. 38(1) (2013), pp. 17–29.

Salman, S. 'The Ethiopian Renaissance Dam: Opportunities & Challenges,' *Sudanow Magazine* (20 September 2013), retrieved from http://sudanow.info.sd/the-ethiopian-renaissance-dam-opportunities-challenges/.

Salman, S. 'Entry into Force of the UN Watercourses Convention: Why Should it Matter?,' *International Journal of Water Resources Development*, Vol. 31(1) (2015), pp. 4–16. DOI:10.1080/07900627.2014.952072.

Salman, S. 'How and Why Has the Ethiopian Strategy on the Renaissance Dam Succeeded?,' *Sudan Vision* (25 May 2015), retrieved from http://news.sudanvisiondaily.com/details.html?rsnpid=248051.

Salman, S. 'The Grand Ethiopian Renaissance Dam: The Road to the Declaration of Principles and the Khartoum Document,' *Water International* Vol. 41(4) (2016), pp. 512–527.

Schwelb, E., 'Fundamental Change of Circumstances,' *in*, *Comments on the 1968 Draft Convention on the Law of Treaties*, pp. 39–70 (Heidelberg: Max-Planck-Institut für ausländisches öffentliches Recht und Völkerrecht, 1999), retrieved from http://www.zaoerv.de/29_1969/29_1969_1_c_39_70.pdf.

Scobbie, I. 'Tom Franck's Fairness,' *European Journal of International Law*, Vol. 13(4) (2002), pp. 909–925.

Shaw, M. 'The Heritage of States: The Principle of uti possidetis juris Today,' *British Yearbook of International Law*, Vol. 67(1) (1996), pp. 75–154.

Shelton, D. 'Equity,' *in*, D. Bodansky, J. Brunnée & E. Hey (eds.), *The Oxford Handbook of International Environmental Law*, pp. 640–661 (Oxford: Oxford University Press, 2007).

Shetewy, M. A. 'Legal Commitments Regulating the Establishment of Water Projects on International Rivers Application Study over the Nile Basin,' *African Perspectives*, Vol. 11(39) (2013), pp. 29–35.

'Sudan to Build Power Transmission Line from Ethiopia's GERD: Minister,' *Sudan Tribune* (28 October 2016), retrieved from http://www.sudantribune.com/spip.php?article60680.

Sutcliffe, J. V., & Y. P. Parks, *The Hydrology of the Nile* (Wallingford: IAHS Press, 1999), retrieved from http://www.hydrosciences.fr/sierem/produits/biblio/hydrology%20of%20the%20Nile.pdf.

Tadele, Y. 'EEPCo, Chinese Company Ink Billion Dollar Transmission Line Deal,' *Fortune*, Vol. 13(678) (28 April 2013).

Tasioulas, J. 'International Law and the Limits of Fairness,' *European Journal of International Law*, Vol. 13(4) (2002), pp. 993–1023.

Tawfik, R. 'The Grand Ethiopian Renaissance Dam: A Benefit-sharing Project in the Eastern Nile?,' *Water International*, Vol. 41(4) (2016), pp. 574–592.

The Covenant of the League of Nations, 28 April 1919.

The Diversion of Water from Meuse (Netherlands v Belgium), PCIJ Series A/B No 70 (28 June 1937).

The Grand Ethiopian Renaissance Dam—A Symbol of Regional Integration, Ventures Africa (4 March 2014), retrieved from http://www.ventures-africa.com/archives/40137.

The Grand Ethiopian Renaissance Dam Fact Sheet, International Rivers Network, retrieved from http://www.internationalrivers.org/resources/the-grand-ethiopian-renaissance-dam-fact-sheet-8213.

The Helsinki Rules on the Uses of the Waters of International Rivers, August 1966, International Law Association.

'The International Law Commission Draft Articles on the Law of the Non-navigational Uses of International Watercourses 1994,' International Legal Commission, retrieved from http://legal.un.org/ilc/texts/instruments/english/commentaries/8_3_1994.pdf.

The Marrakesh Agreement Establishing the World Trade Organization, 1994, 1869 *UNTS* 299.

Treaties between the United Kingdom and Ethiopia, and between the United Kingdom, Italy, and Ethiopia, relative to the frontiers between the Soudan, Ethiopia and Eritrea, Addis Ababa, 15 May 1902, retrieved from http://treaties.fco.gov.uk/docs/pdf/1902/TS0016.pdf.

Tvedt, T. *The River Nile in the Post-colonial Age: Conflict and Cooperation in the Nile Basin Countries* (London: I. B. Tauris & Co, 2009).

Ulfstein, G. 'Reweaving the Fabric of International Law? Patters of Consent in Environmental Framework Agreements,' *in*, R. Wolfrum & V. Roben (eds.), *Developments of International Law in Treaty Making*, pp. 145–154 (Heidelberg: Springer, 2005).

United Arab Republic and Sudan Agreement (with Annexes) for the Full Utilization of the Nile Waters, 8 November 1959.

Universal Declaration on Human Rights, 10 December 1948, Resolution 217 A(III), United Nations General Assembly.

Van Hoof, G. J. H. *Rethinking the Sources of International Law* (Berlin: Kluwer, 1983).

Veilleux, J. 'The Human Security Dimensions of Dam Development: The Grand Ethiopian Renaissance Dam,' *Global Dialogue*, Vol. 15(2) (2013), retrieved from http://www.transboundarywaters.orst.edu/publications/publications/Veilleux_GLOBAL%20DIALOGUE_V15_GERD.pdf.

Verhoeven, H. 'Africa's Next Hegemon: Behind Ethiopia's Power Plays,' *Foreign Affairs* (12 April 2015), retrieved from https://www.foreignaffairs.com/articles/ethiopia/2015-04-12/africas-next-hegemon.

Vienna Convention on the Law of Treaties, 23 May 1969, 1155 *UNTS* 331.

Wahish, N. 'Toshka Turns Millennial Green,' *Al-Ahram Weekly On-line*, Issue No. 392 (27 August–2 September 1998), retrieved from http://weekly.ahram.org.eg/archive/1998/392/ec1.htm.

Waldoc, Sir H., 'First Report on the Law of Treaties,' *in*, *Yearbook of the International Law Commission 1962, Vol. II*, pp. 27–80 (New York: United Nations, 1964), retrieved from http://legal.un.org/ilc/publications/yearbooks/english/ilc_1962_v2.pdf.

Wheeler, K. G. et al, 'Cooperative Filling Approaches for the Grand Ethiopian Renaissance Dam,' *Water International*, Vol. 41(4) (2016), pp. 611–634.

Whittington, D., J. Waterbury & M. Jeuland, 'The Grand Renaissance Dam and Prospects for Cooperation on the Eastern Nile,' *Water Policy*, Vol. 16(4) (2014), pp. 595–608. DOI: 10.2166/wp.2014.011.

Woldetsadik, T. W. *International Watercourses Law in the Nile River Basin: Three States at a Crossroads* (Abingdon: Routledge, 2013).

Wolfrum, R. 'Commentary on Purposes and Principles (Art 1),' *in*, B. Simma et al, *The Charter of the United Nations: A Commentary, 3rd ed., Volume 1*, pp. 113–114 (Oxford: Oxford University Press, 2012).

World Commission on Dams, *Dams and Development—A New Framework for Decision-making* (London: Earthscan, 2000), p. 167.

Wouters, P. *International Water Law: Selected Writings of Professor Charles B. Bourne* (Leiden: Martinus Nijhoff, 1997).

Yigzaw, Z. A. *Open Letter to Egypt: A Response to The Spokesman of Egypt's Ministry of Foreign Affairs Regarding the GERDP from An Ethiopian Perspective*, Abbay Nile (28 March 2014), retrieved from https://zenileabbay.wordpress.com/2014/03/28/open-letter-to-egypt-a-response-to-the-spokes-man-of-egypts-ministry-of-foreign-affairs-regarding-gerdp-from-an-ethiopian-perspective/.

Yihdego, Z. 'Arms Control and Human Security: What Role for NSAs?,' *in*, C. Ryngaert & M. Noortmann, *Human Security and International Law: The Challenge of Non-State Actors*, pp. 135–174 (Cambridge: Intersentia, 2014).

Yihdego, Z. *The Blue Nile Dam Controversy in the Eyes of International Law*, Global Water Forum, retrieved from http://www.globalwaterforum.org/2013/06/18/the-blue-nile-dam-controversy-in-the-eyes-of-international-law/.

Yihdego, Z., & A. Rieu-Clarke, 'An Exploration of Fairness in International Law Through the Blue Nile and GERD,' *Water International*, Vol. 41(4) (2016), pp. 528–549.

Yihdego, Z., A. Rieu-Clarke & A. Cascão, 'How Has the Grand Ethiopian Renaissance Dam Changed the Legal, Political, Economic and Scientific Dynamics in the Nile Basin?,' *Water International*, Vol. 41(4) (2106), pp. 503–511.

Zaher, A. 'Egypt-Ethiopia Tension Set to Rise,' *The Arab Weekly*, Issue 78 (23 October 2016).

Zhang, Y., S. Erkyihum & P. Block, 'Filling the GERD: Evaluating Hydroclimatic Variability and Impoundment Strategies for Blue Nile Riparian Countries,' *Water International*, Vol. 41(4) (2016), pp. 593–610.

www.ingramcontent.com/pod-product-compliance
Lightning Source LLC
Chambersburg PA
CBHW031332230926
51848CB00001B/204
* 9 7 8 9 0 0 4 3 5 1 7 5 2 *